SPRING Journal

Name: & Age:

Address:

Phone & Email:

INSTRUCTIONS

LIST or DRAW NINE THINGS
That you want to learn about:

1.
2.
3.
4.
5.
6.
7.
8.
9.

Action Steps:

1. Go to the library or bookstore.
2. Bring home a stack of at least NINE interesting books about these topics. Choose some that have diagrams, instructions and illustrations.

Supplies Needed:

You will need pencils, colored pencils, pens and markers.

You can change books or add new books at anytime.
Record extra books in the back.

Choose Nine Books To Use As School Books!

1. Write down the titles on each cover below.
2. Keep your stack of books in a safe place.
3. Be ready to read a few pages from your books daily.
4. Complete 6 to 8 pages each day in this workbook.

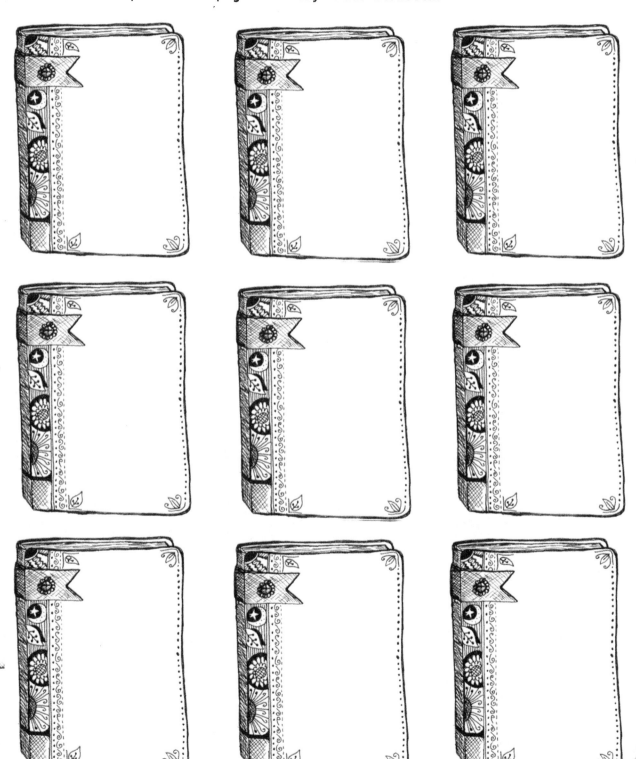

What do you want to do today?

Today's Date:_____

Copy a Verse or Quote

_____
_____
_____
_____
_____

My Plans:

_____
_____
_____
_____

To-Do List

_____
_____
_____
_____
_____
_____

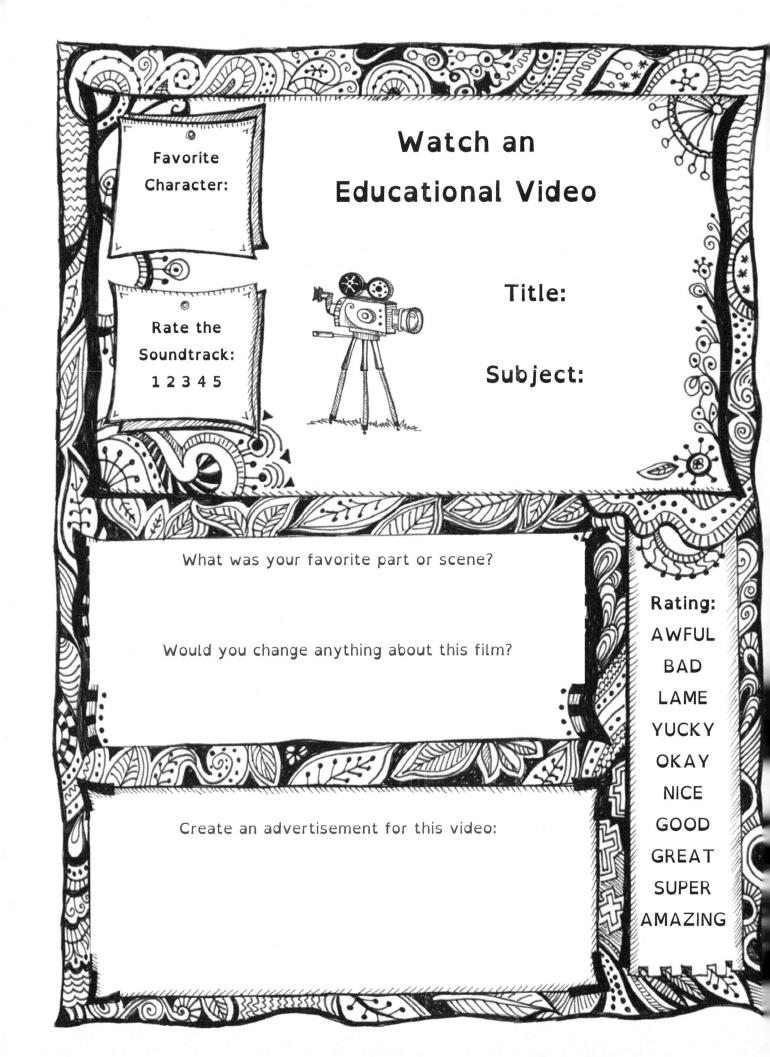

Color me with colored pencils.
Write just one word to describe me:

_____

Write Today's Date: _____

Color the picture and write a story about it.

How are you feeling today?
Color the facial expression

The look on a person's face can help you understand how they feel.

Creative Writing

Reading Time - 1 Hour (Set a timer)

Choose Four Books - Read from each book for 15 minutes.
Copy important words or pictures from each book here:

Spelling Time

Find 20 Words with 4 letters each.
Look in your books for words.
Write the words here:

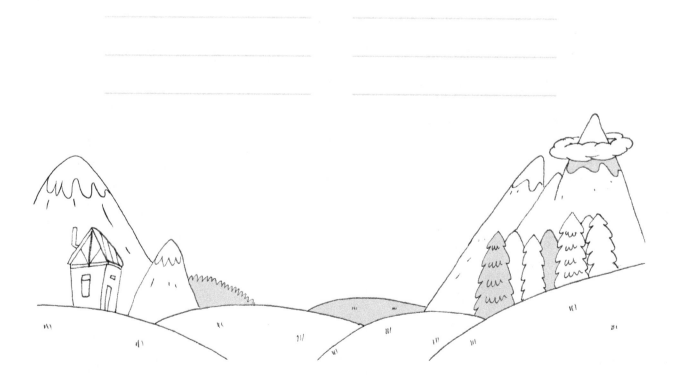

Thinking Time!

Can you complete the puzzle?

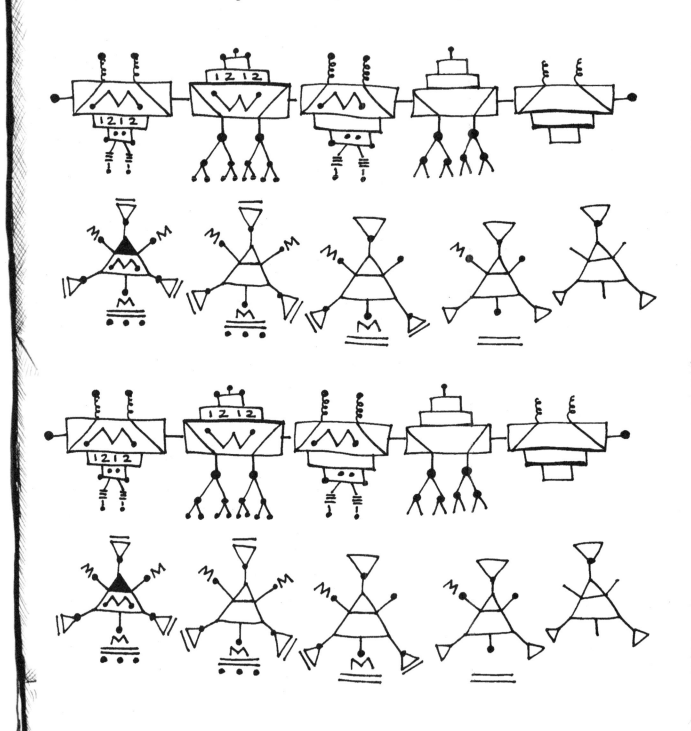

What do you want to do today?

LETTER DOODLES

Practice working with your colored pencils and learn to draw amazing letters too!

Object Lesson

Look at this picture.
List four things that you
can do with this object.

1. _____
2. _____
3. _____
4. _____

World News Today!

Talk to your parents about current events.
Look at a newspaper, news broadcast or website.
Tell the news stories with words and pictures.

WHO:

WHAT:

WHEN:

WHERE:

WHY:

Book Time

Find an interesting sentence in one of your books and copy it. Draw a picture to go with the words.

TITLE:_____

Page Number:_____

Write Today's Date:_____

Color the picture and write a story about it.

Reading Time - 1 Hour (Set a timer)

Choose Four Books - Read from each book for 15 minutes.

Copy important words or pictures from each book here:

Spelling Time

Find 20 Words with 5 letters each.
Look in your books for words.
Write the words here:

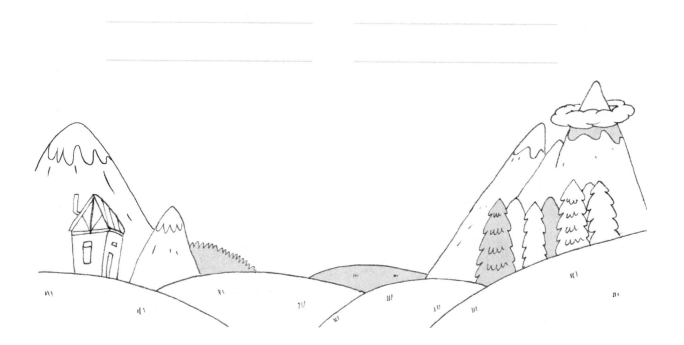

Today's Date:_____

Copy a Verse or Quote

_____
_____
_____
_____
_____

My Plans:

_____
_____
_____
_____

To-Do List

_____
_____
_____
_____
_____
_____

LETTER DOODLES

Practice working with your colored pencils and learn to draw amazing letters too!

Object Lesson

Look at this picture.
List four things that you
can do with this object.

1. _____
2. _____
3. _____
4. _____

How are you feeling today?
Color the facial expressions that match your mood.

Color me with colored pencils.
Write just one word to describe me:

_____

Creative Writing

_____
_____
_____
_____
_____
_____
_____

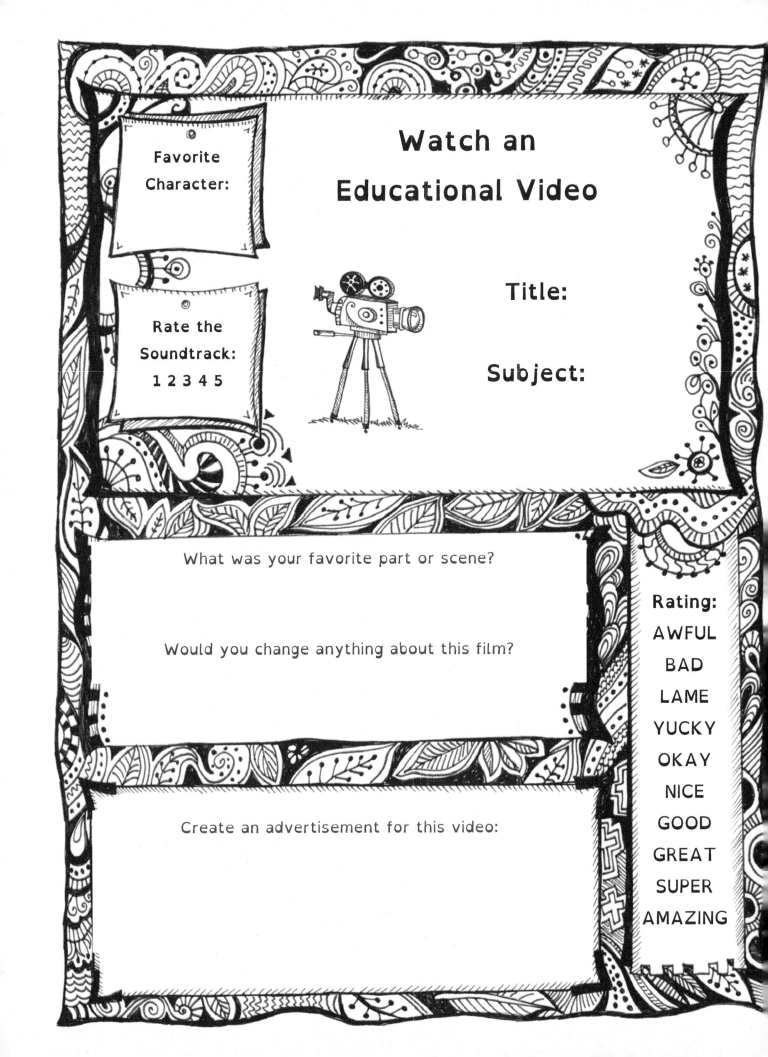

Use THIS PAGE for Math Practice
Or be creative and design something, like a house! You could make graphs, maps or geometric designs with this graph paper.

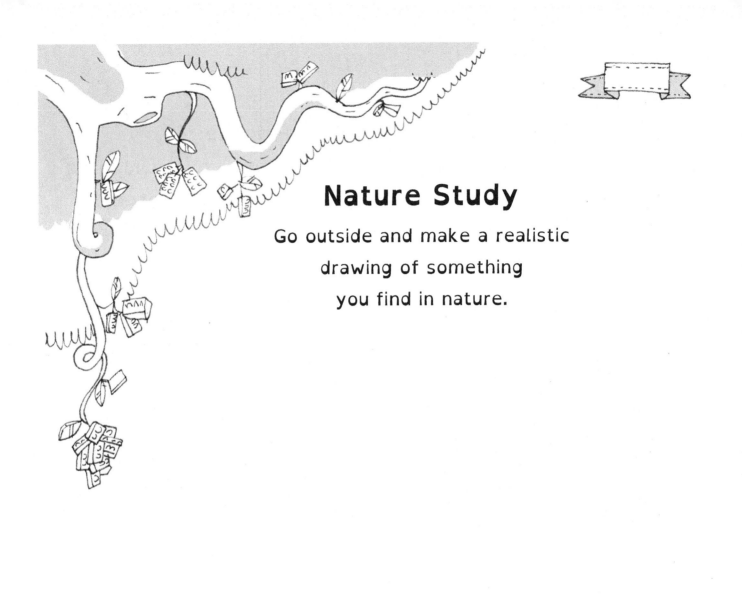

Nature Study

Go outside and make a realistic drawing of something you find in nature.

Reading Time - 1 Hour (Set a timer)

Choose Four Books - Read from each book for 15 minutes.

Copy important words or pictures from each book here:

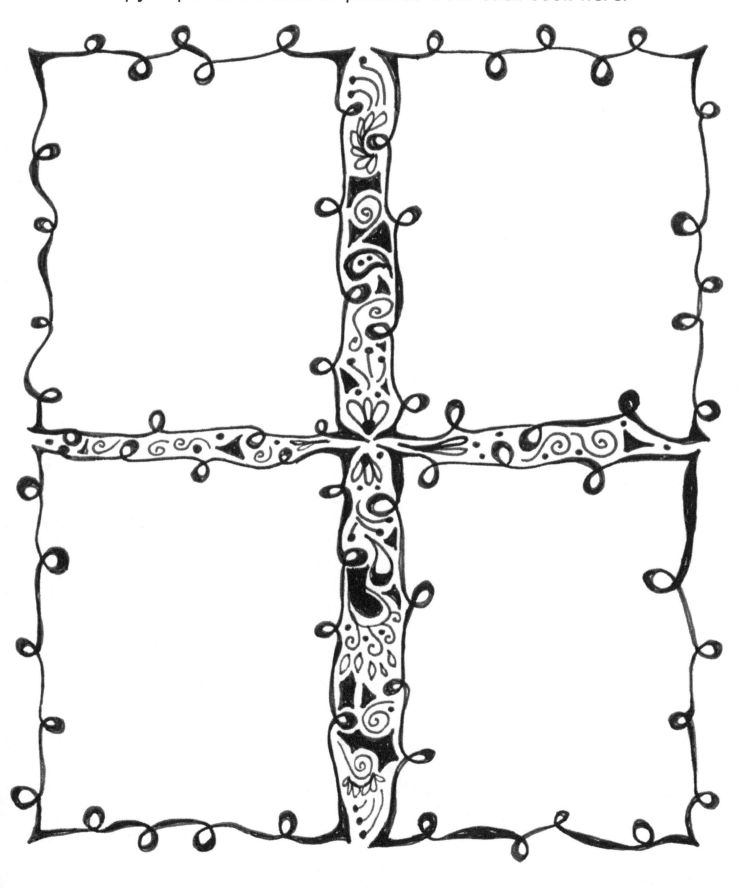

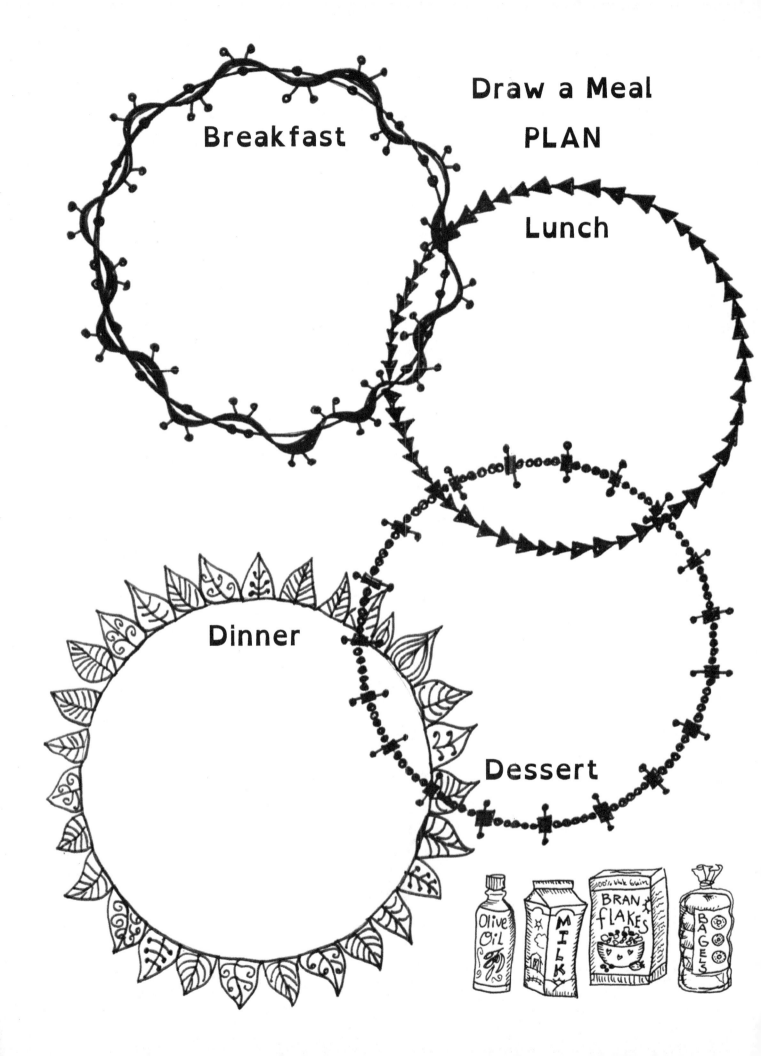

Book Time

Find an interesting sentence in one of your books and copy it. Draw a picture to go with the words.

TITLE:_____

Page Number:_____

Animal Quiz

How much do you know about this animal?

Can you draw the animal's habitat, food and enemies?

Thinking Time!

Can you complete the puzzle?

Write Today's Date:_____

Color the picture and write a story about it.

This page is blank, unlike your mind.
Fill this page with words or rhymes.
Use the space for doodle dreams.
Make a list or draw something.

Today's Date:_____

Copy a Verse or Quote

My Plans:

To-Do List

LETTER DOODLES

Practice working with your colored pencils and learn to draw amazing letters too!

Object Lesson

Look at this picture.
List four things that you
can do with this object.

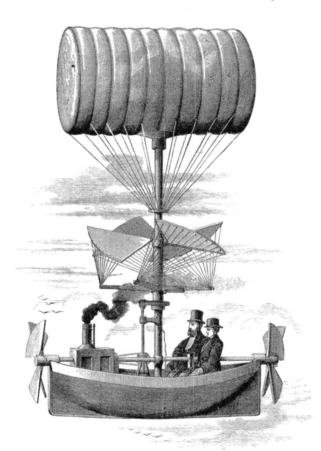

1. _____
2. _____
3. _____
4. _____

How are you feeling today?
Color the facial expression

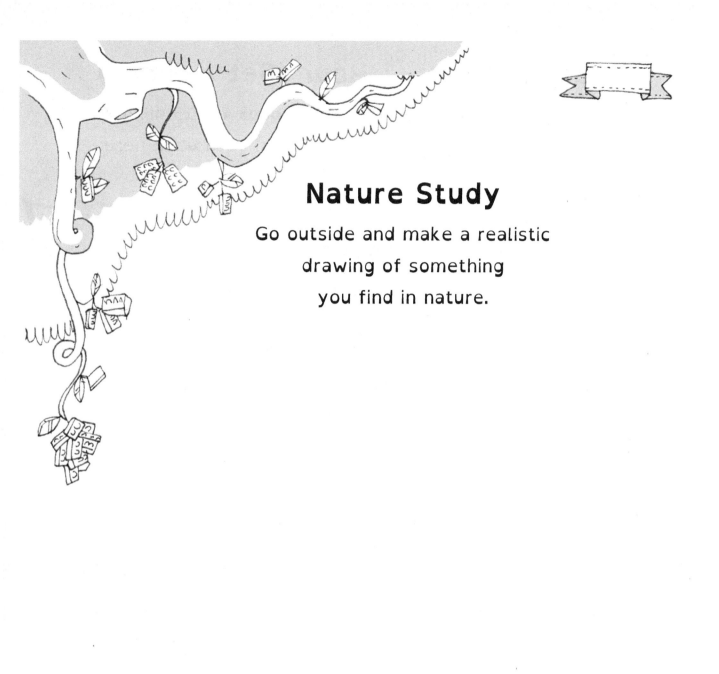

Nature Study

Go outside and make a realistic drawing of something you find in nature.

Reading Time - 1 Hour (Set a timer)

Choose Four Books - Read from each book for 15 minutes.

Copy important words or pictures from each book here:

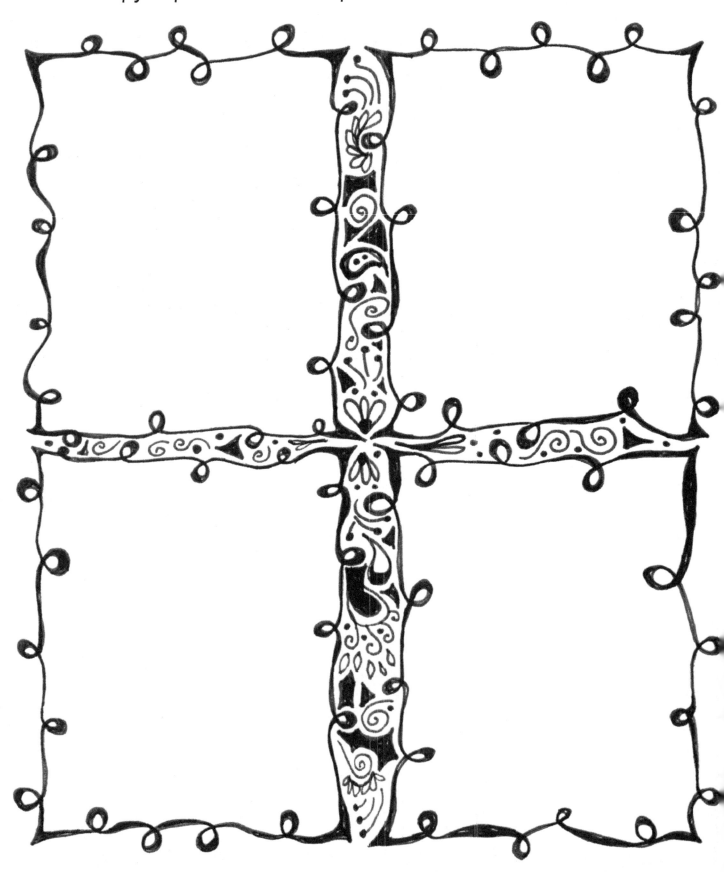

Spelling Time

Find 20 Words with 6 letters each.
Look in your books for words.
Write the words here:

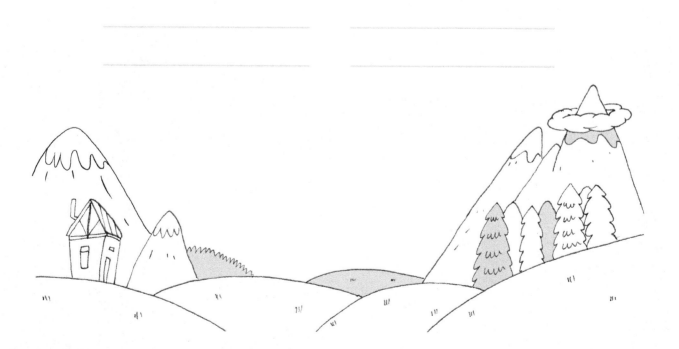

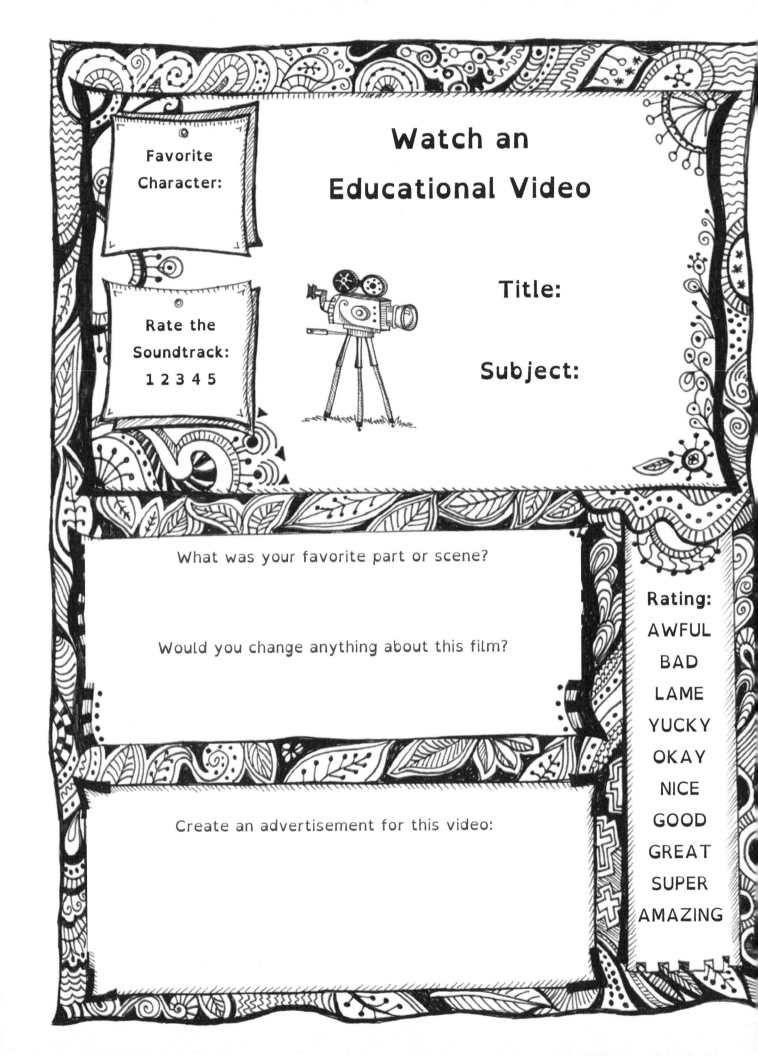

Animal Quiz

How much do you know about this animal?

Can you draw the animal's habitat, food and enemies?

Use THIS PAGE for Math Practice

Or be creative and design something, like a house! You could make graphs, maps or geometric designs with this graph paper.

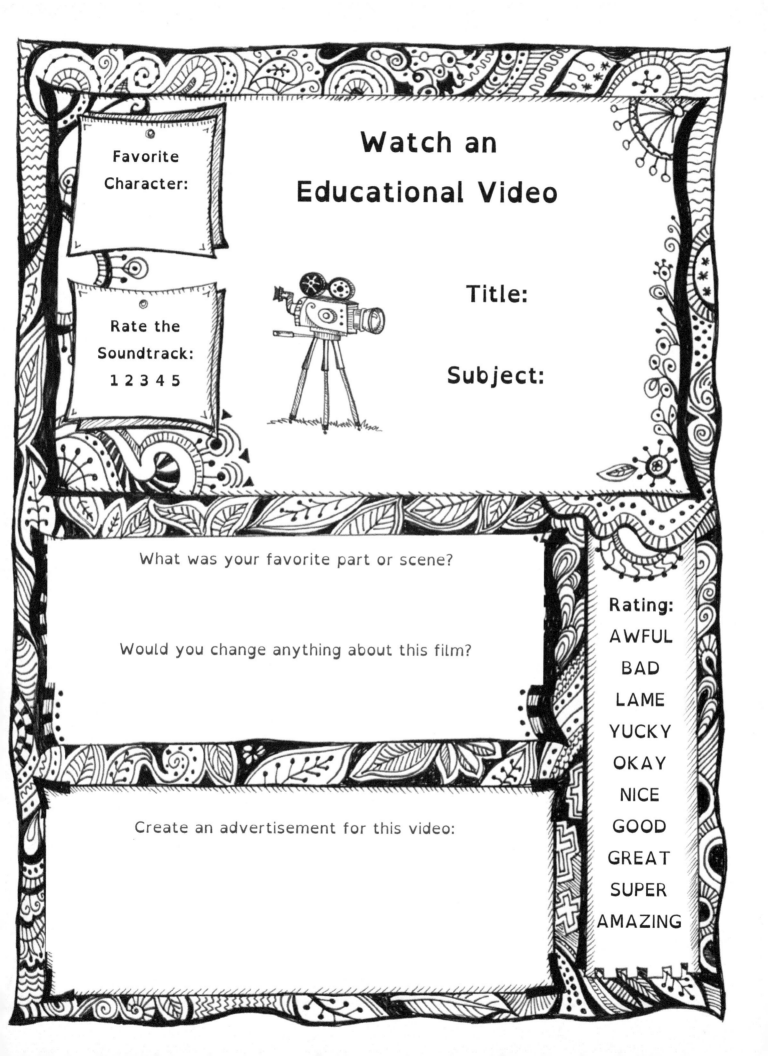

Book Time

Find an interesting sentence in one of your books and copy it. Draw a picture to go with the words.

TITLE: _____

Page Number: _____

Thinking Time!

Can you complete the puzzle?

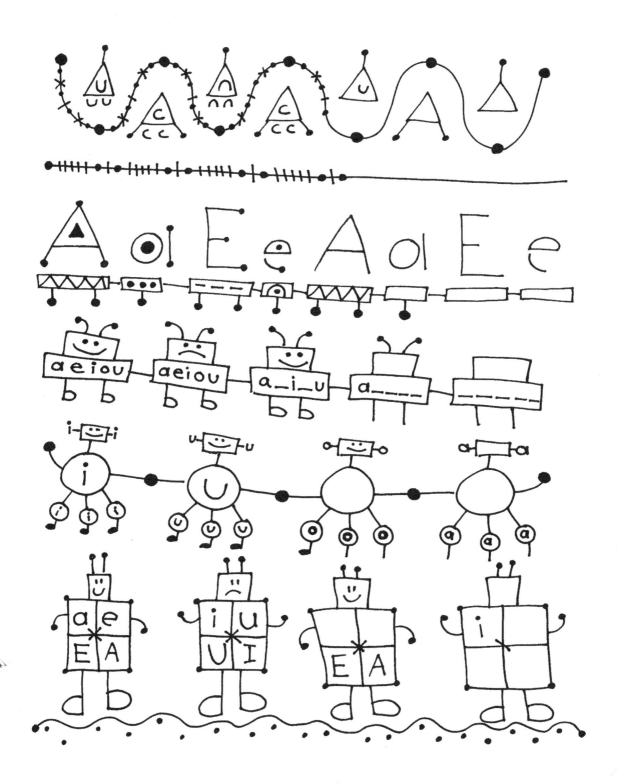

This page is blank, unlike your mind.
Fill this page with words or rhymes.
Use the space for doodle dreams.
Make a list or draw something.

Today's Date:_____

Copy a Verse or Quote

My Plans:

To-Do List

LETTER DOODLES

Practice working with your colored pencils and learn to draw amazing letters too!

Object Lesson

Look at this picture.
List four things that you
can do with this object.

1. _____
2. _____
3. _____
4. _____

Write Today's Date:_____

Color the picture and write a story about it.

How are you feeling today?
Color the facial expressions that match your mood.

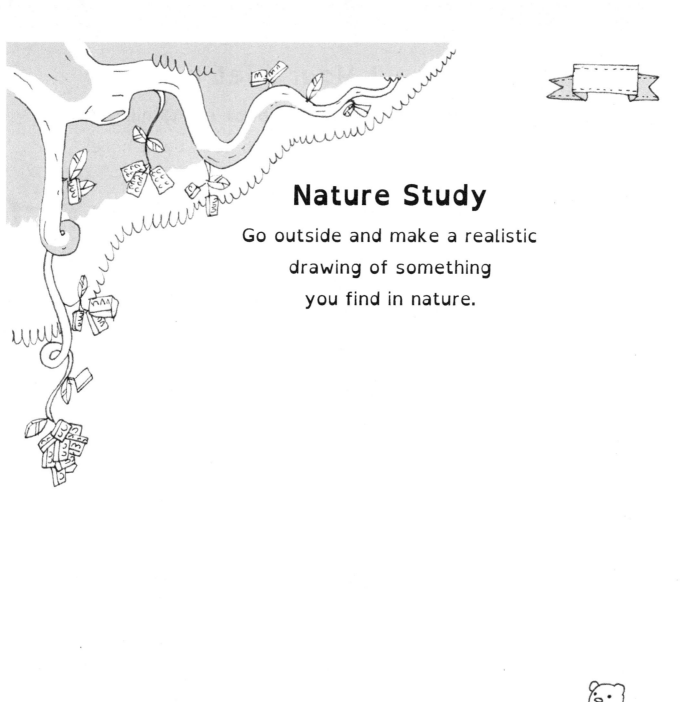

Nature Study

Go outside and make a realistic drawing of something you find in nature.

Reading Time - 1 Hour (Set a timer)

Choose Four Books - Read from each book for 15 minutes.

Copy important words or pictures from each book here:

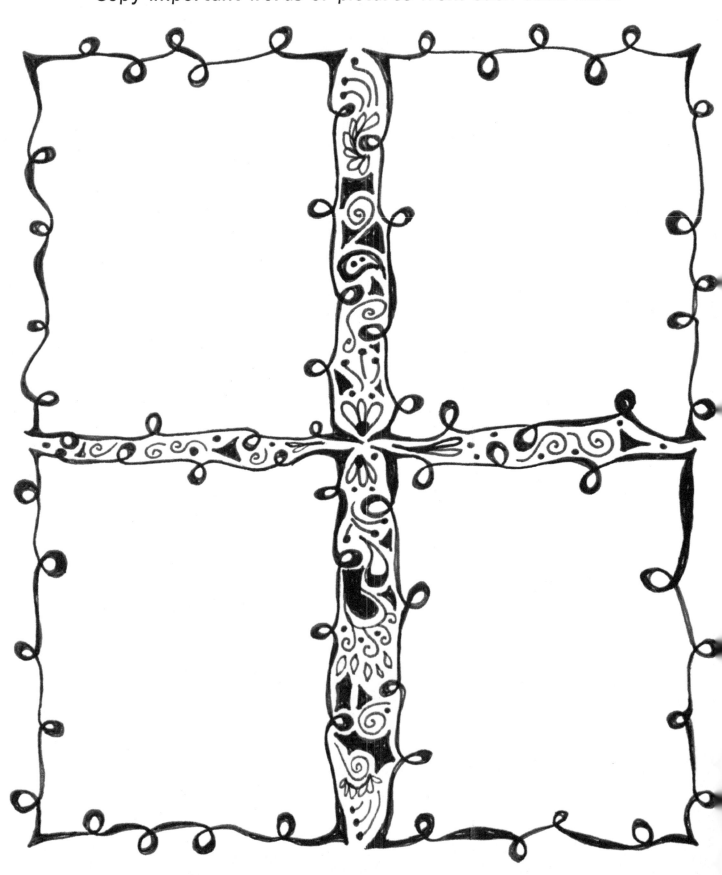

Spelling Time

Find 20 Words with 7 letters each.
Look in your books for words.
Write the words here:

_____   _____
_____   _____
_____   _____
_____   _____
_____   _____
_____   _____
_____   _____
_____   _____
_____   _____
_____   _____

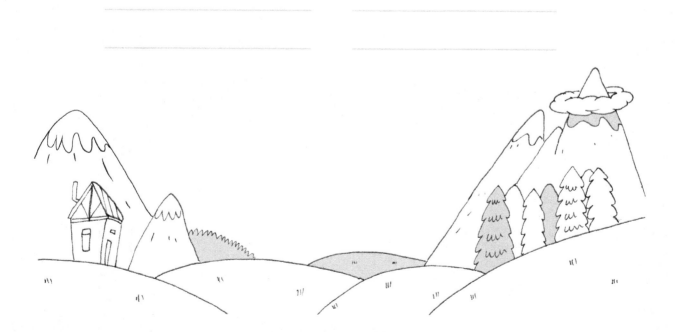

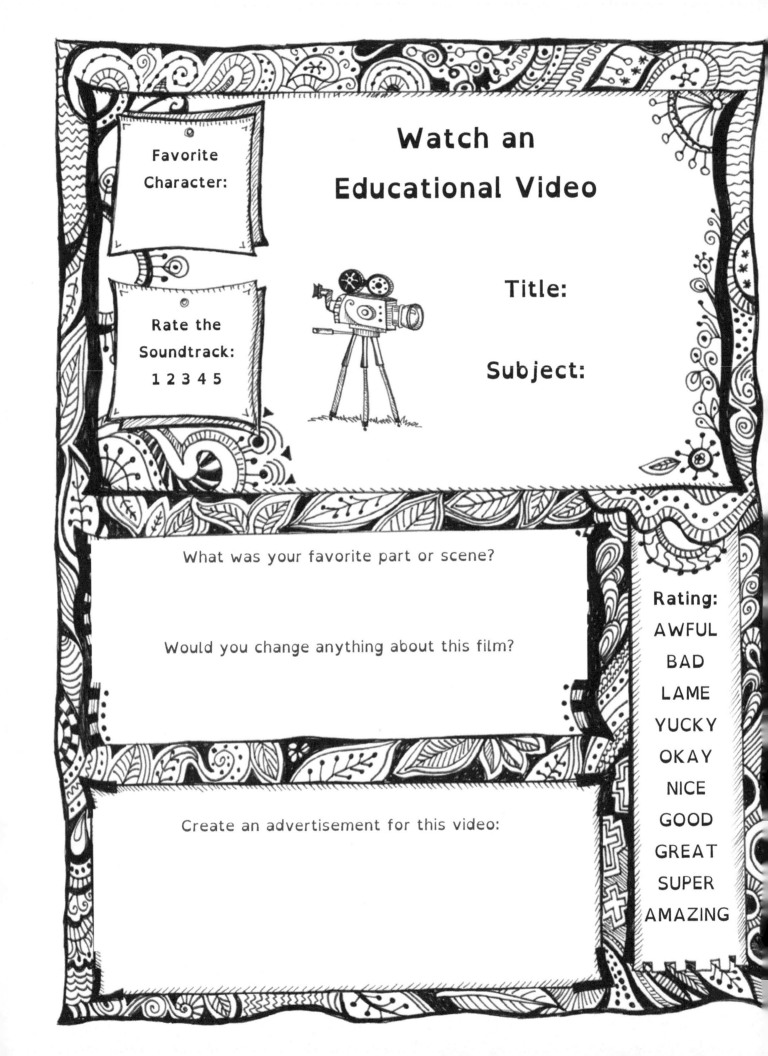

Use THIS PAGE for Math Practice
Or be creative and design something, like a house! You could make graphs, maps or geometric designs with this graph paper.

Book Time

Find an interesting sentence in one of your books and copy it. Draw a picture to go with the words.

TITLE: _____

Page Number: _____

Color me with colored pencils.
Write just one word to describe me:

_____

Write Today's Date: _____

Color the picture and write a story about it.

Thinking Time!

Can you complete the puzzle?

This page is blank, unlike your mind.
Fill this page with words or rhymes.
Use the space for doodle dreams.
Make a list or draw something.

LETTER DOODLES

Practice working with your colored pencils and learn to draw amazing letters too!

Object Lesson

Look at this picture.
List four things that you
can do with this object.

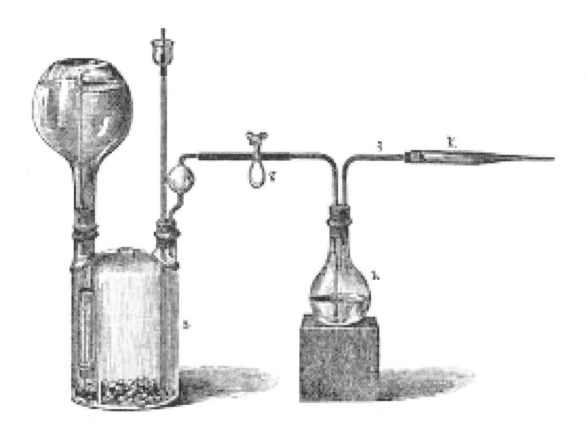

1. _____
2. _____
3. _____
4. _____

How are you feeling today?
Circle all the facial expressions that best depict your moods today.

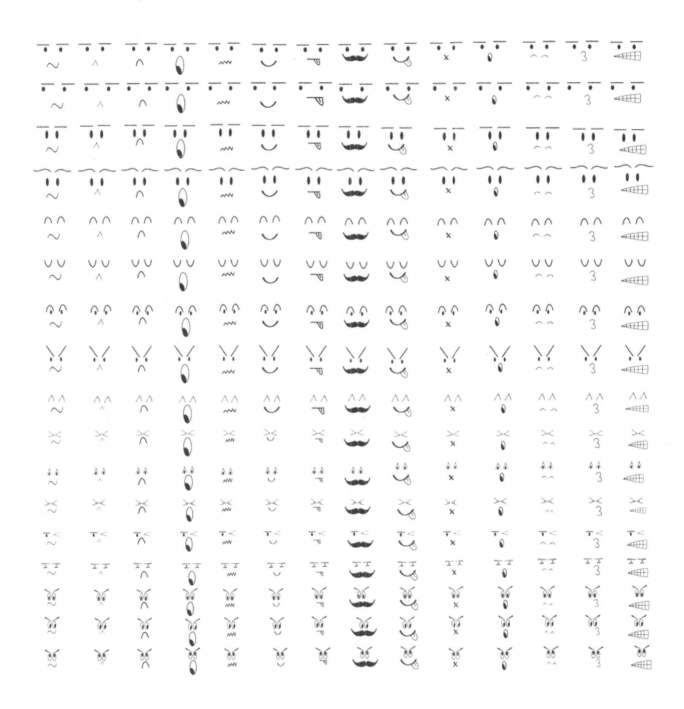

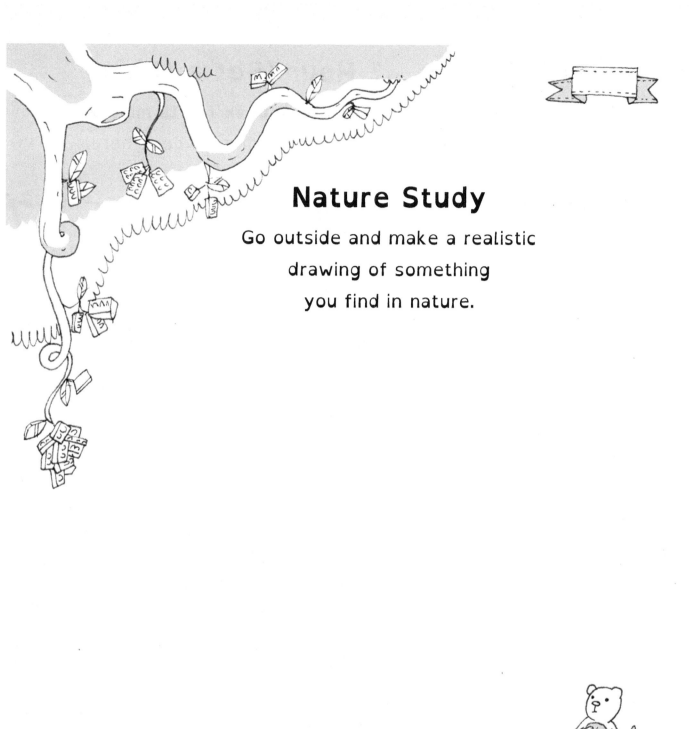

Nature Study

Go outside and make a realistic drawing of something you find in nature.

Reading Time - 1 Hour (Set a timer)

Choose Four Books - Read from each book for 15 minutes.

Copy important words or pictures from each book here:

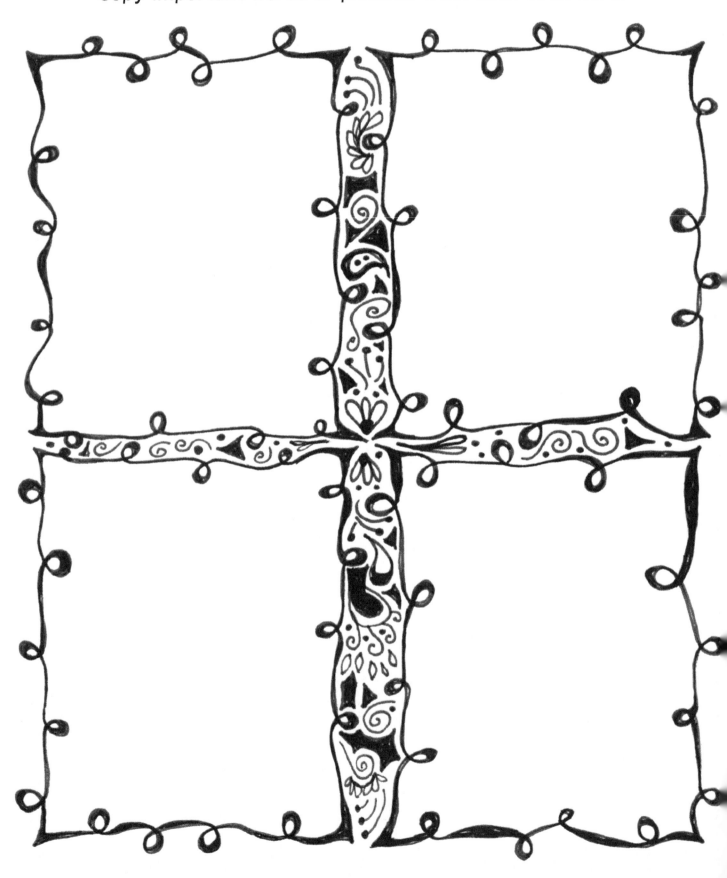

Animal Quiz

How much do you know about this animal?

Can you draw the animal's habitat, food and enemies?

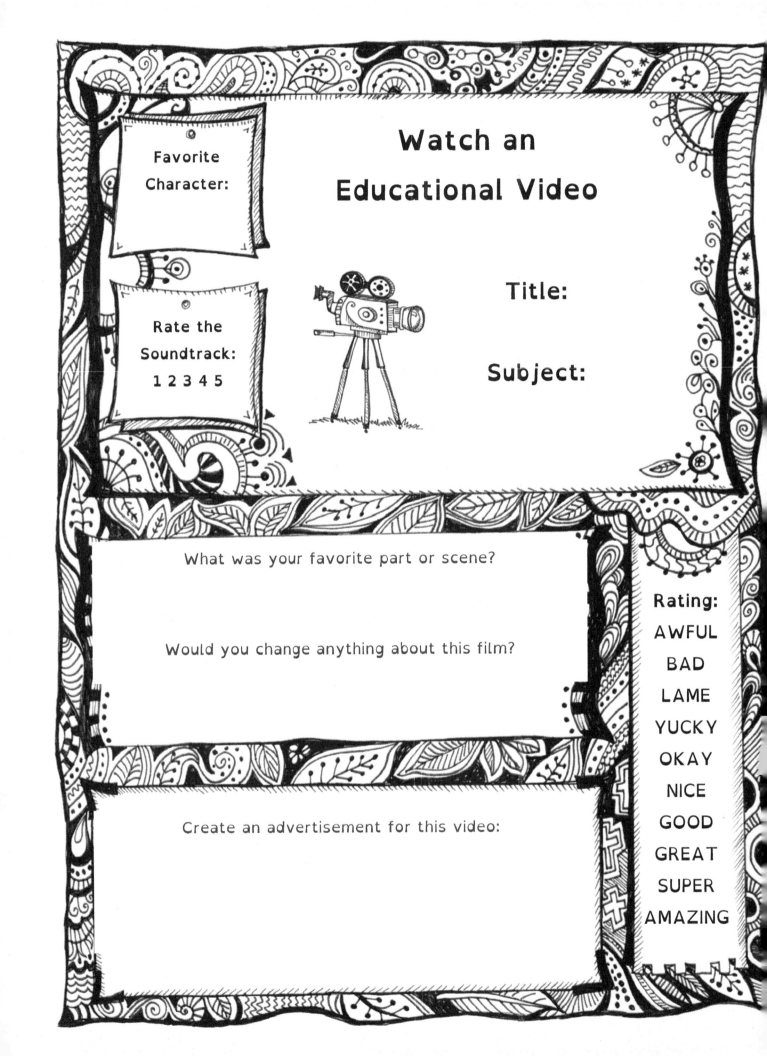

Use THIS PAGE for Math Practice
Or be creative and design something, like a house! You could make graphs, maps or geometric designs with this graph paper.

Write Today's Date:_____

Color the picture and write a story about it.

Listening Time

Listen to an audio book or classical music or ask someone to read a story to you while you color and draw on the next page.

What are you listening to?

_____

Thinking Time!

Can you complete the puzzle?

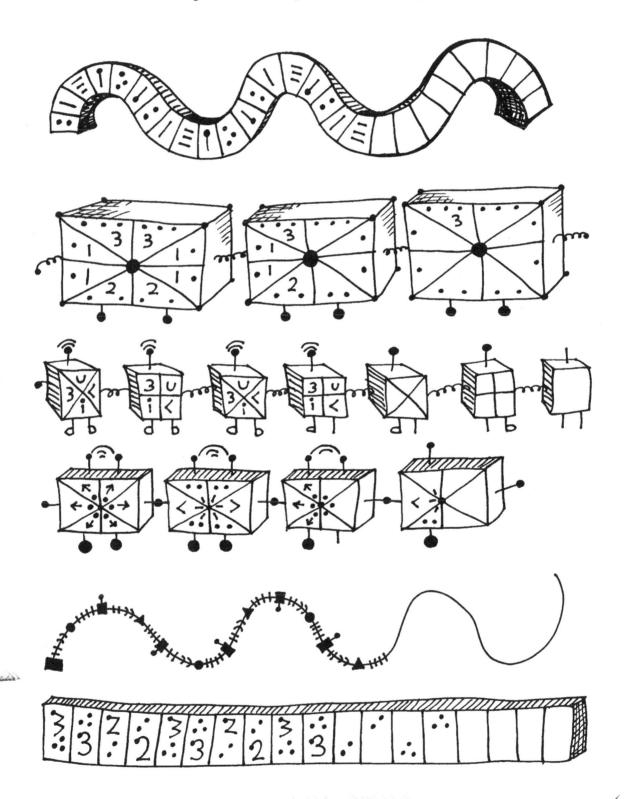

Color me with colored pencils.

Write just one word to describe me:

Today's Date:_____

Copy a Verse or Quote

_____
_____
_____
_____
_____

My Plans:

_____
_____
_____
_____

To-Do List

_____
_____
_____
_____
_____
_____

LETTER DOODLES

Practice working with your colored pencils and learn to draw amazing letters too!

Object Lesson

Look at this picture.
List four things that you
can do with this object.

1. _____
2. _____
3. _____
4. _____

How are you feeling today?
Color the facial expressions that match your mood.

Nature Study

Go outside and make a realistic
drawing of something
you find in nature.

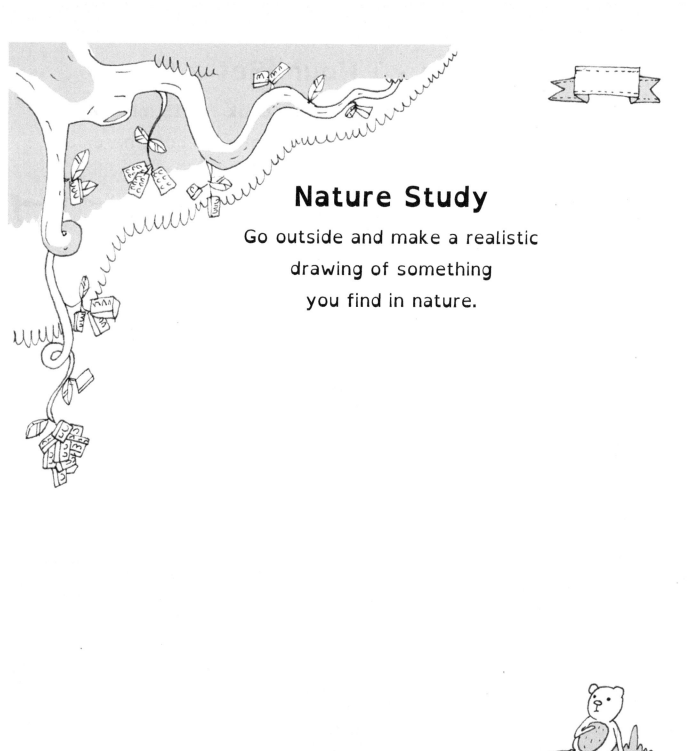

Reading Time - 1 Hour (Set a timer)

Choose Four Books - Read from each book for 15 minutes.

Copy important words or pictures from each book here:

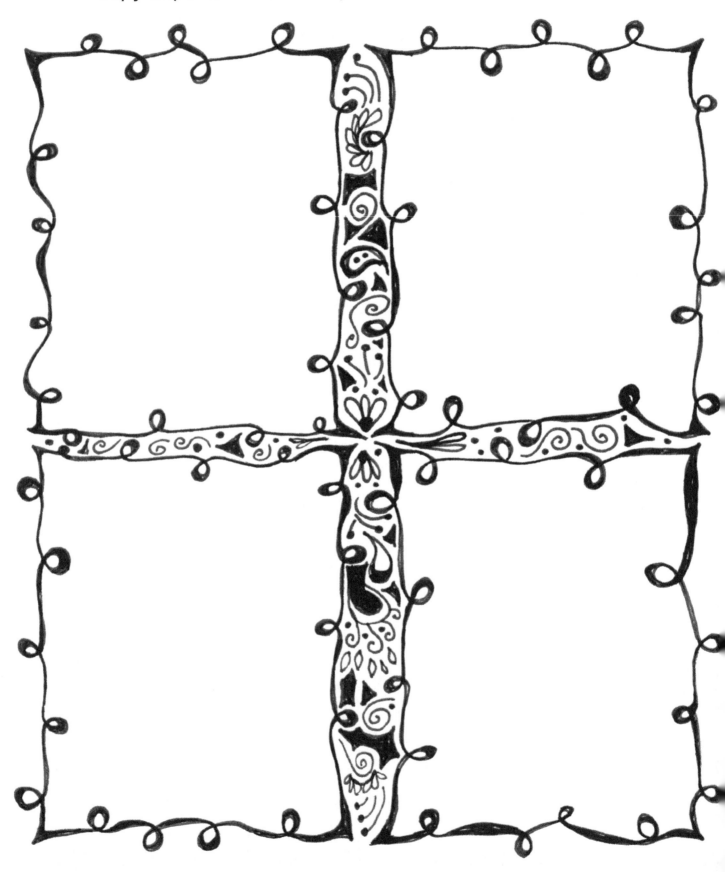

Spelling Time

Find 20 Words with 9 letters each.
Look in your books for words.
Write the words here:

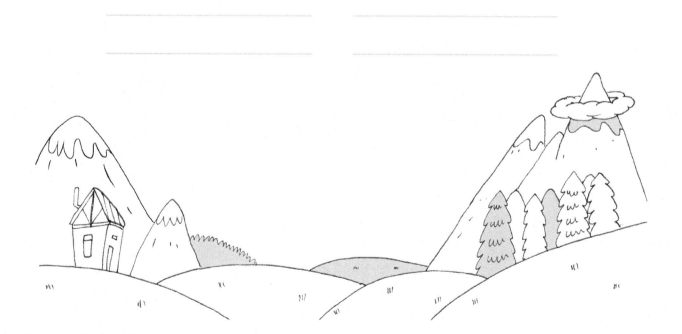

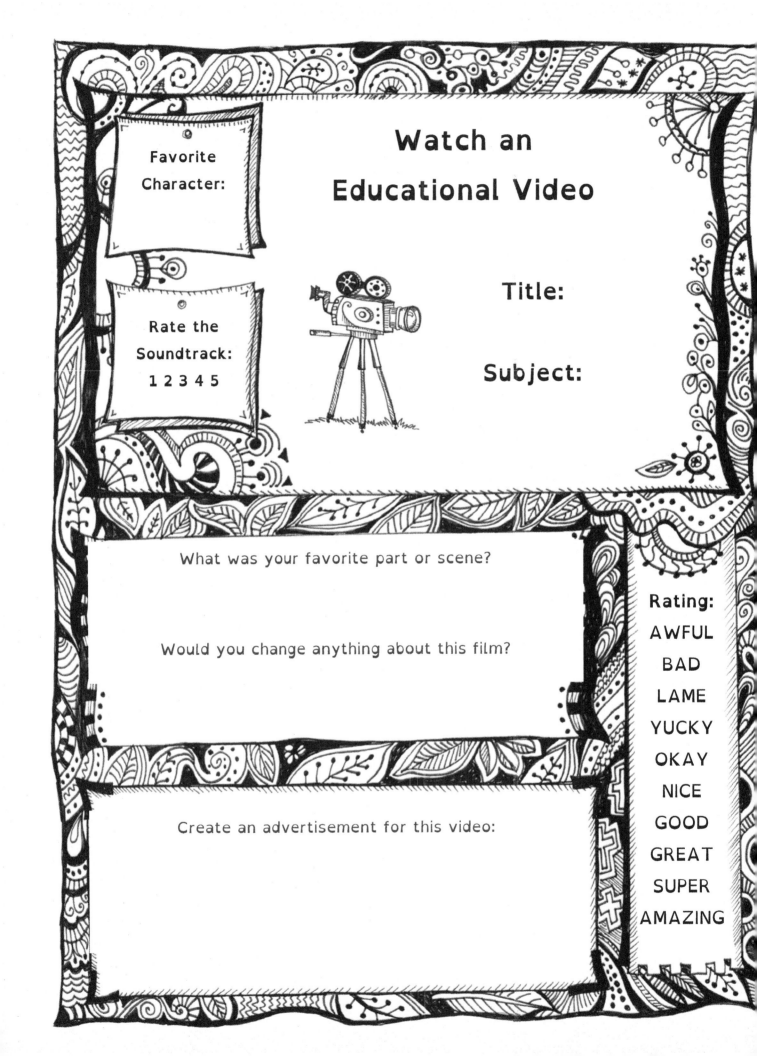

Use THIS PAGE for Math Practice

Or be creative and design something, like a house! You could make graphs, maps or geometric designs with this graph paper.

World News Today!

Talk to your parents about current events.
Look at a newspaper, news broadcast or website.
Tell the news stories with words and pictures.

WHO:

WHAT:

WHEN:

WHERE:

WHY:

Book Time

Find an interesting sentence in one of your books and copy it. Draw a picture to go with the words.

TITLE:_____

Page Number:_____

Thinking Time!

Can you complete the puzzle?

Color me with colored pencils.

Write just one word to describe me:

_____

Today's Date:_____

Copy a Verse or Quote

_____
_____
_____
_____
_____

My Plans:

_____
_____
_____
_____

To-Do List

_____
_____
_____
_____
_____
_____
_____

Write Today's Date:_____

Color the picture and write a story about it.

LETTER DOODLES

Practice working with your colored pencils and learn to draw amazing letters too!

Object Lesson

Look at this picture.
List four things that you
can do with this object.

1. _____
2. _____
3. _____
4. _____

How are you feeling today?
Color the facial expressions that match your mood.

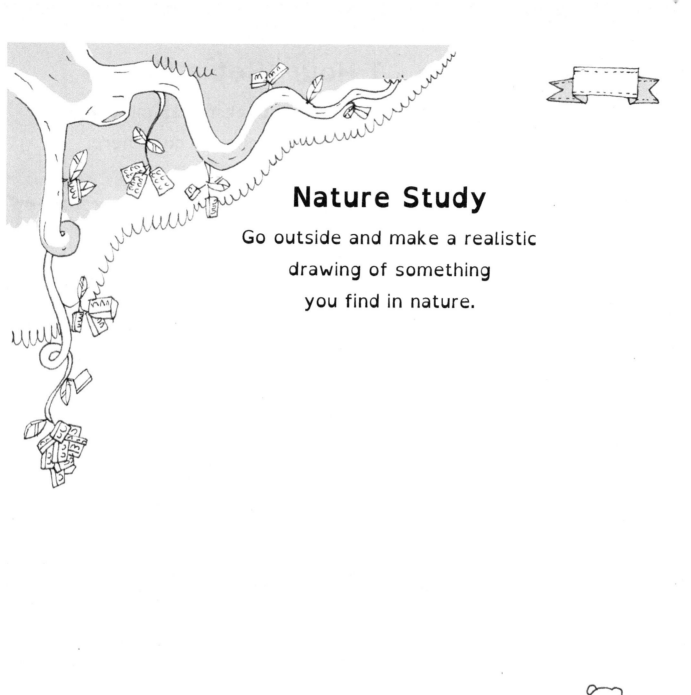

Nature Study

Go outside and make a realistic drawing of something you find in nature.

Reading Time - 1 Hour (Set a timer)

Choose Four Books - Read from each book for 15 minutes.
Copy important words or pictures from each book here:

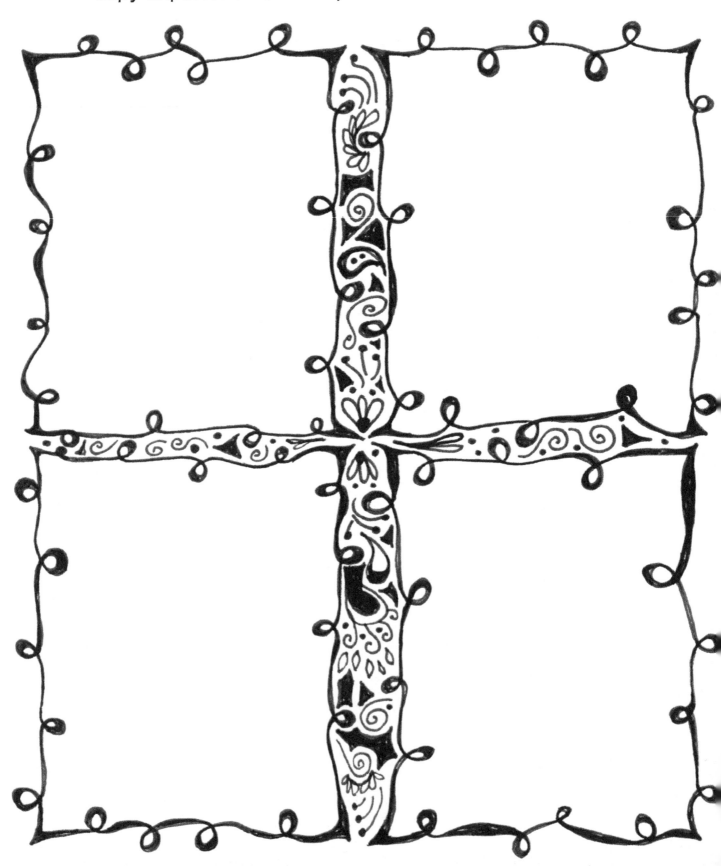

Spelling Time

Find 20 Words with 8 letters each.
Look in your books for words.
Write the words here:

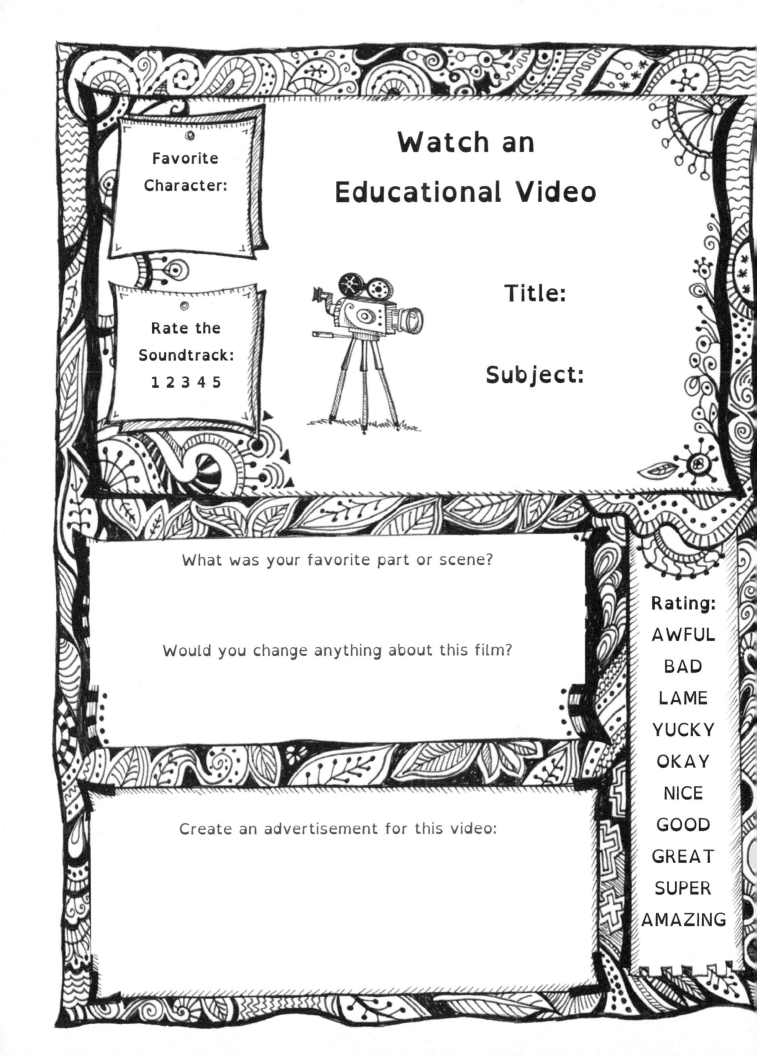

Use THIS PAGE for Math Practice
Or be creative and design something, like a house! You could make graphs, maps or geometric designs with this graph paper.

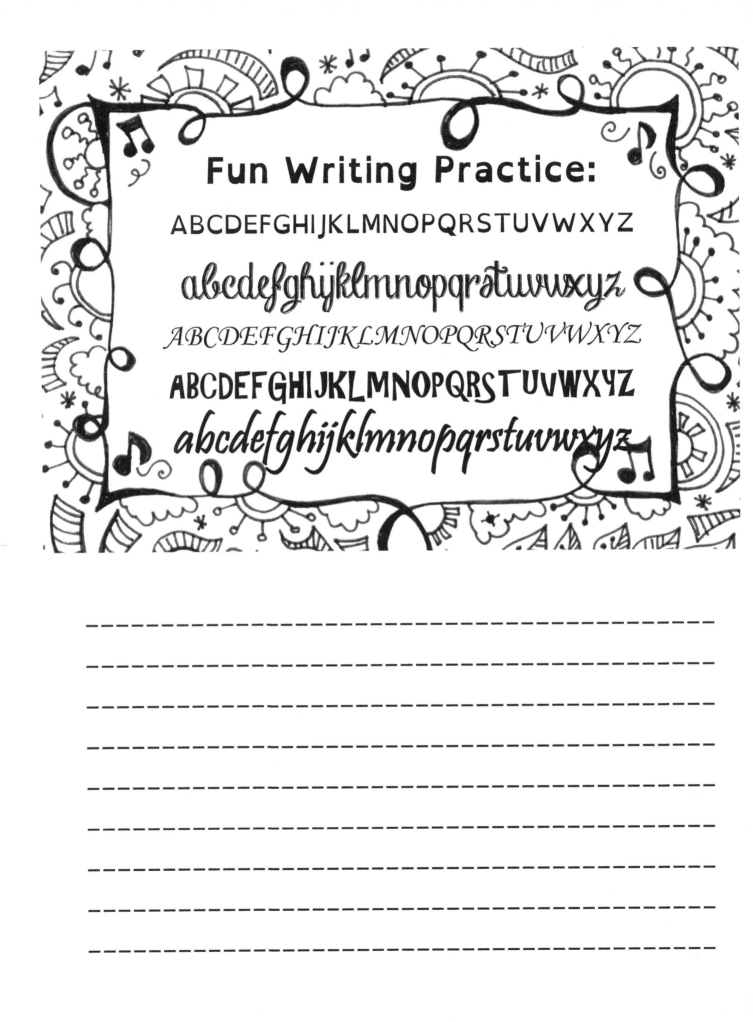

Book Time

Find an interesting sentence in one of your books and copy it. Draw a picture to go with the words.

TITLE:_____

Page Number:_____

Thinking Time!

Can you complete the puzzle?

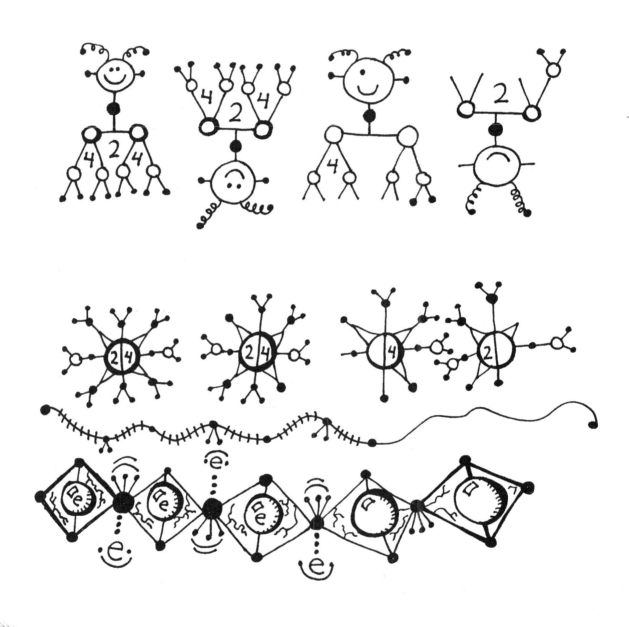

Color me with colored pencils.

Write just one word to describe me:

_____

Today's Date:_____

Copy a Verse or Quote
_____
_____
_____
_____
_____

My Plans:
_____
_____
_____
_____

To-Do List
_____
_____
_____
_____
_____
_____

LETTER DOODLES

Practice working with your colored pencils and learn to draw amazing letters too!

Object Lesson

Look at this picture.
List four things that you
can do with this object.

1. _____
2. _____
3. _____
4. _____

How are you feeling today?
Color the facial expressions that match your mood.

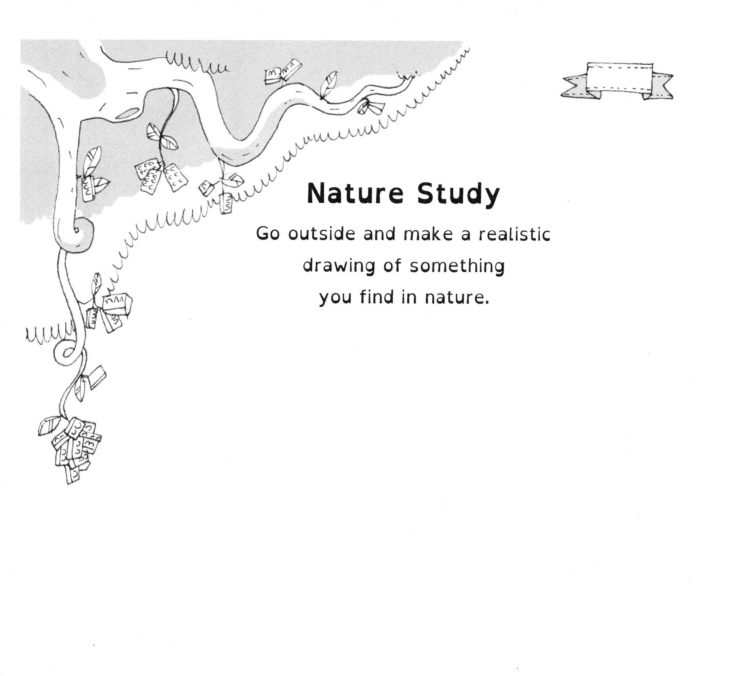

Nature Study

Go outside and make a realistic drawing of something you find in nature.

Write Today's Date: _____

Color the picture and write a story about it.

Reading Time - 1 Hour (Set a timer)

Choose Four Books - Read from each book for 15 minutes.

Copy important words or pictures from each book here:

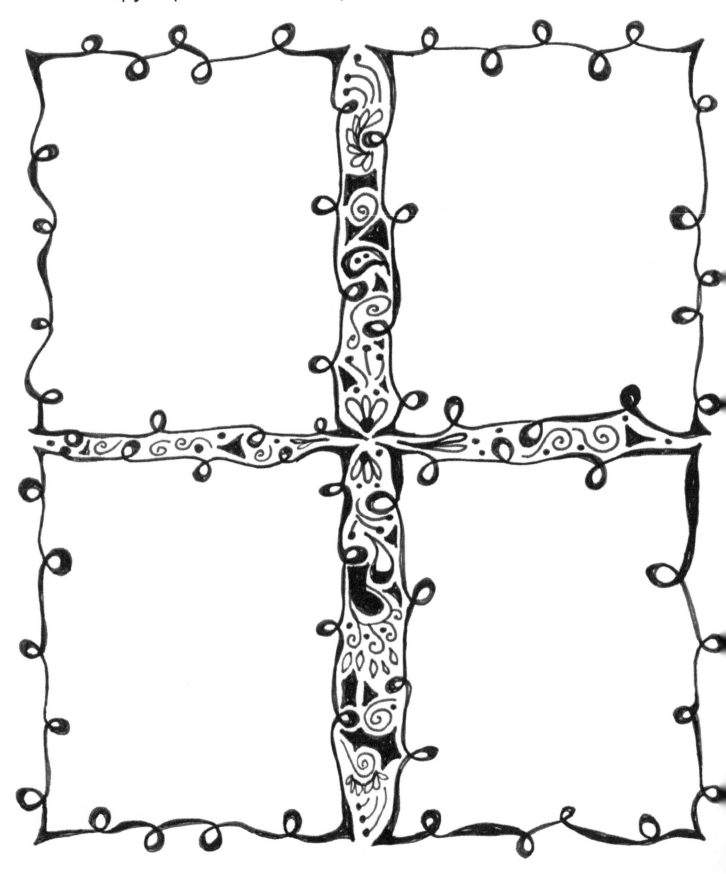

Spelling Time

Find 20 Words with 7 letters each.
Look in your books for words.
Write the words here:

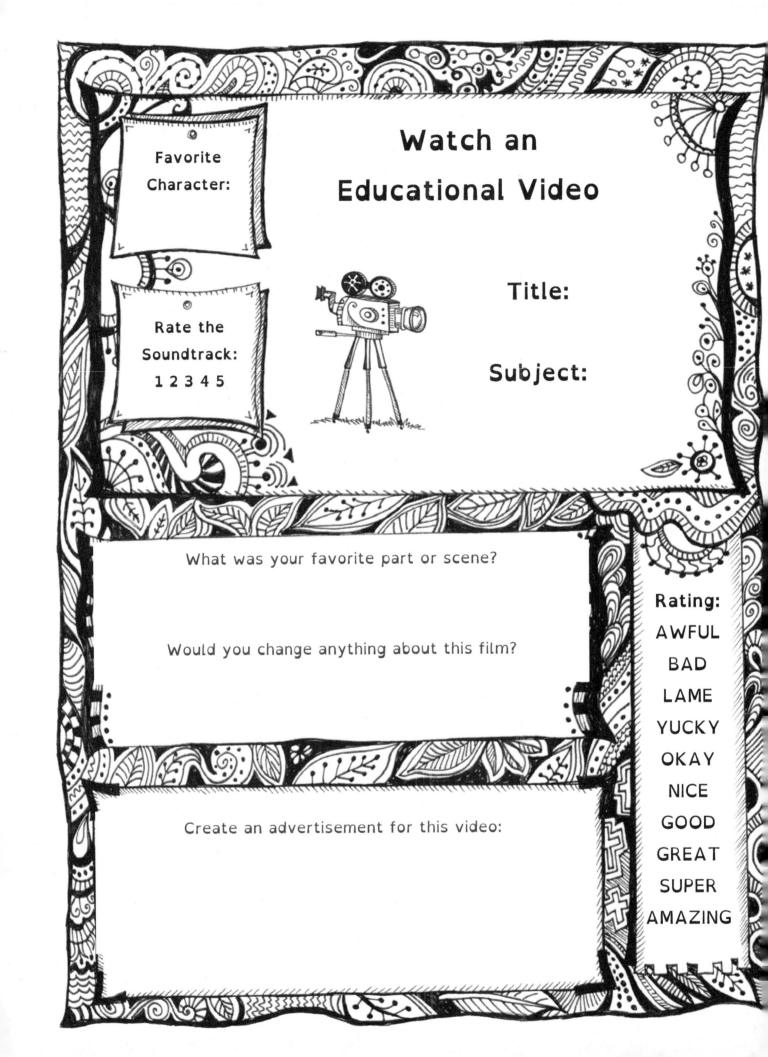

Use THIS PAGE for Math Practice
Or be creative and design something, like a house! You could make graphs, maps or geometric designs with this graph paper.

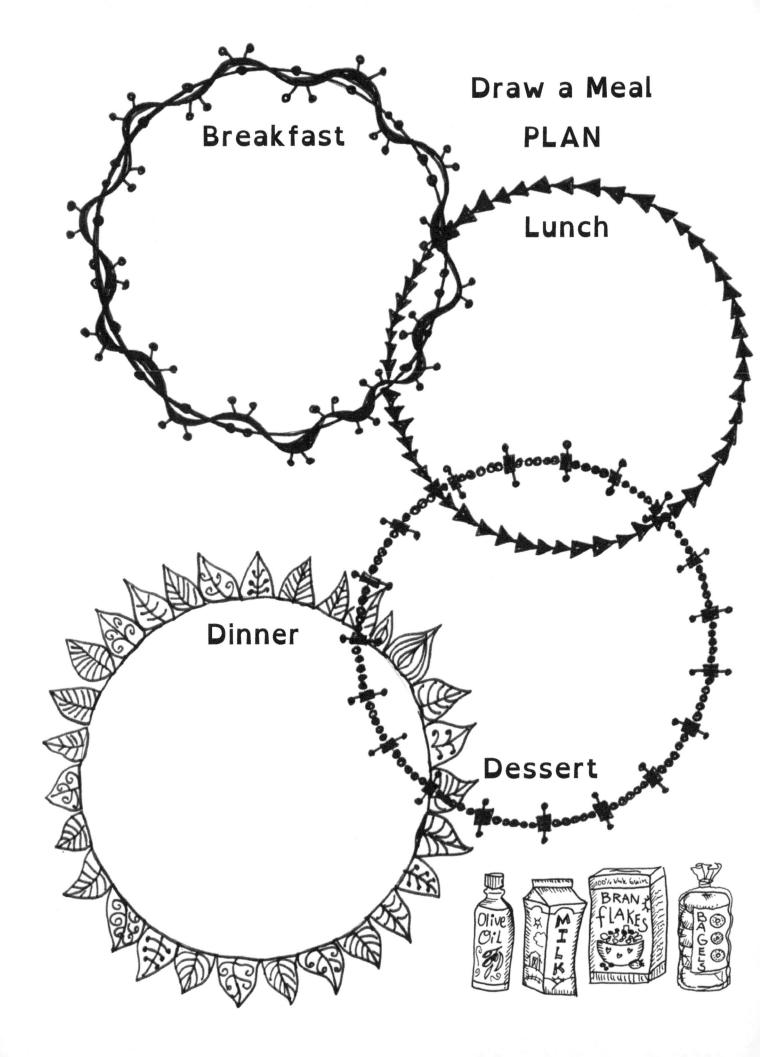

Book Time

Find an interesting sentence in one of your books and copy it. Draw a picture to go with the words.

TITLE:_____

Page Number:_____

Thinking Time!

Can you complete the puzzle?

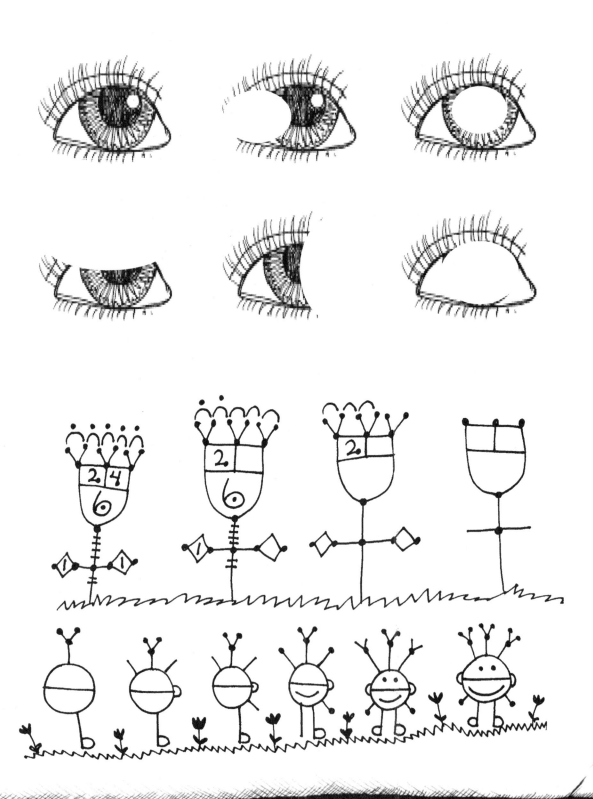

Today's Date:_____

Copy a Verse or Quote

My Plans:

To-Do List

LETTER DOODLES

Practice working with your colored pencils and learn to draw amazing letters too!

Color me with colored pencils.
Write just one word to describe me:

_____

Object Lesson

Look at this picture.
List four things that you
can do with this object.

1. _____
2. _____
3. _____
4. _____

How are you feeling today?
Color the facial expressions that match your mood.

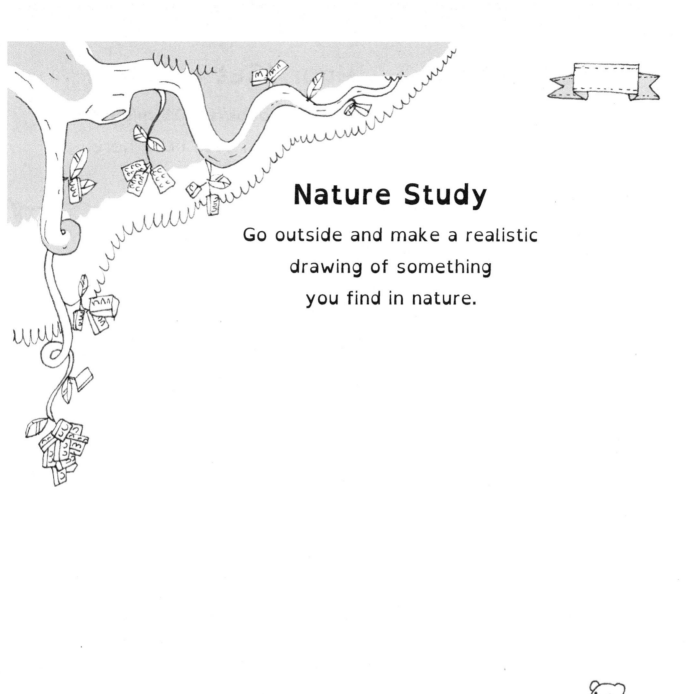

Nature Study

Go outside and make a realistic drawing of something you find in nature.

Reading Time - 1 Hour (Set a timer)

Choose Four Books - Read from each book for 15 minutes.

Copy important words or pictures from each book here:

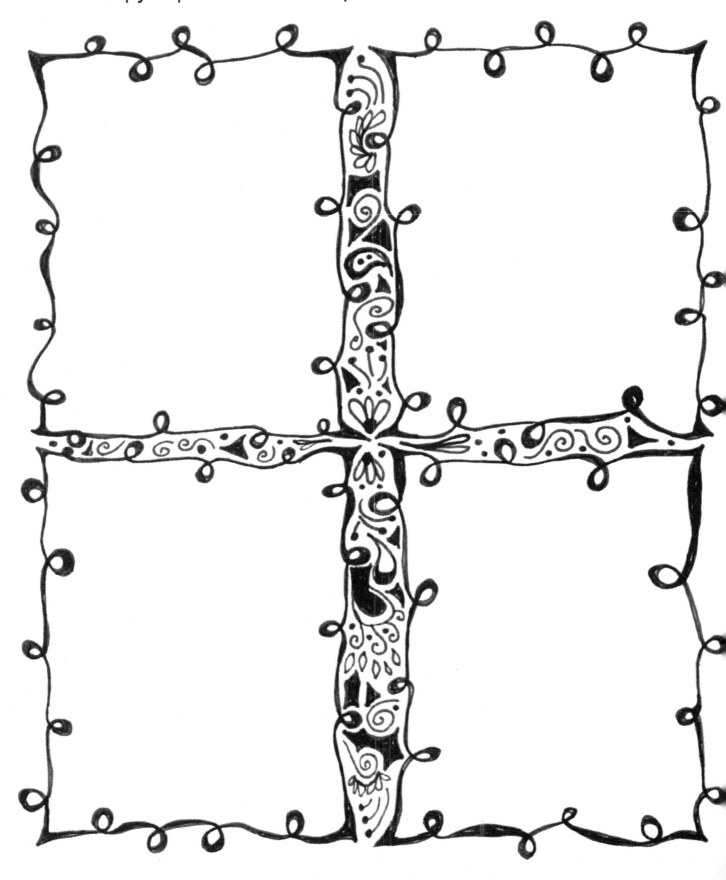

Spelling Time

Find 20 Words with 6 letters each.
Look in your books for words.
Write the words here:

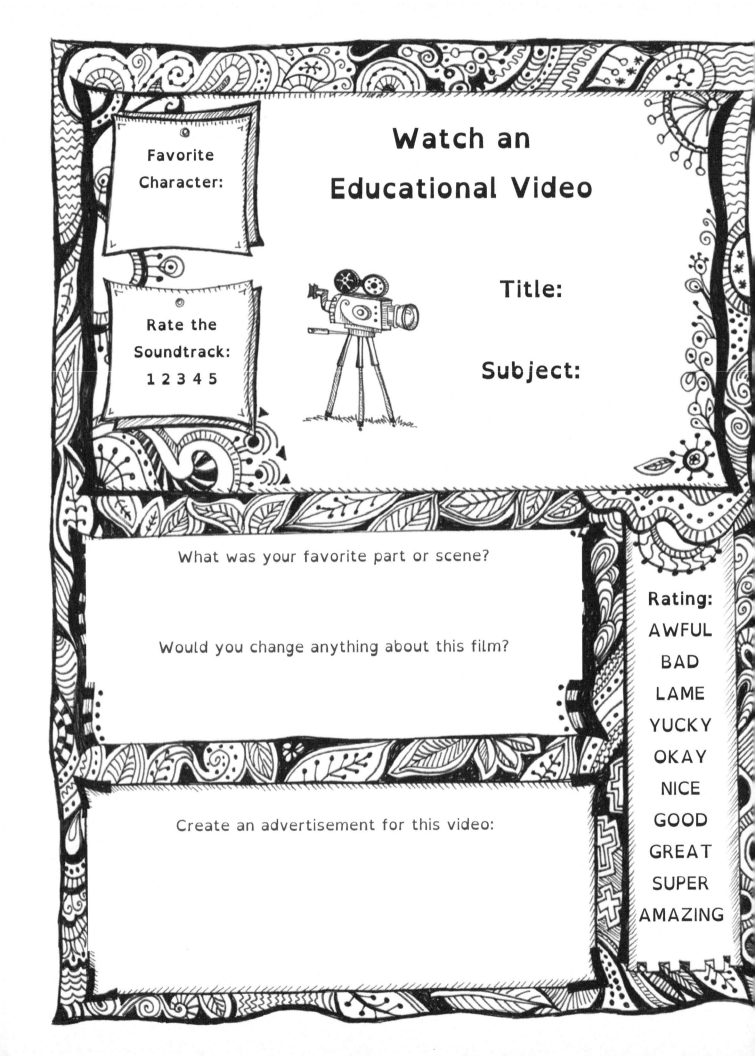

Use THIS PAGE for Math Practice

Or be creative and design something, like a house! You could make graphs, maps or geometric designs with this graph paper.

Book Time

Find an interesting sentence in one of your books and copy it. Draw a picture to go with the words.

TITLE:_____

Page Number:_____

Thinking Time!

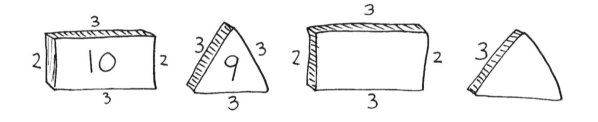

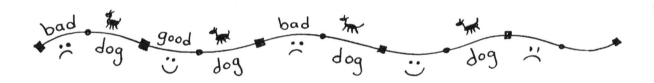

Today's Date:_____

Copy a Verse or Quote

My Plans:

To-Do List

LETTER DOODLES

Practice working with your colored pencils and learn to draw amazing letters too!

Object Lesson

Look at this picture.
List four things that you
can do with this object.

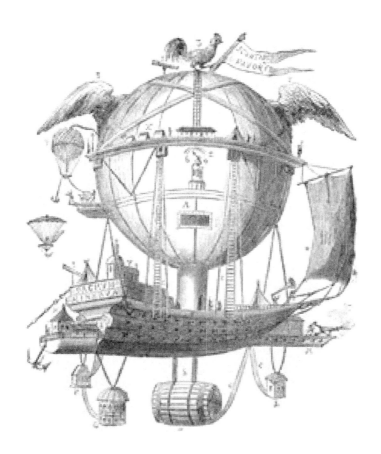

1. _____
2. _____
3. _____
4. _____

Color me with colored pencils.
Write just one word to describe me:

_____

How are you feeling today?
Circle all the facial expressions that best depict your moods today.

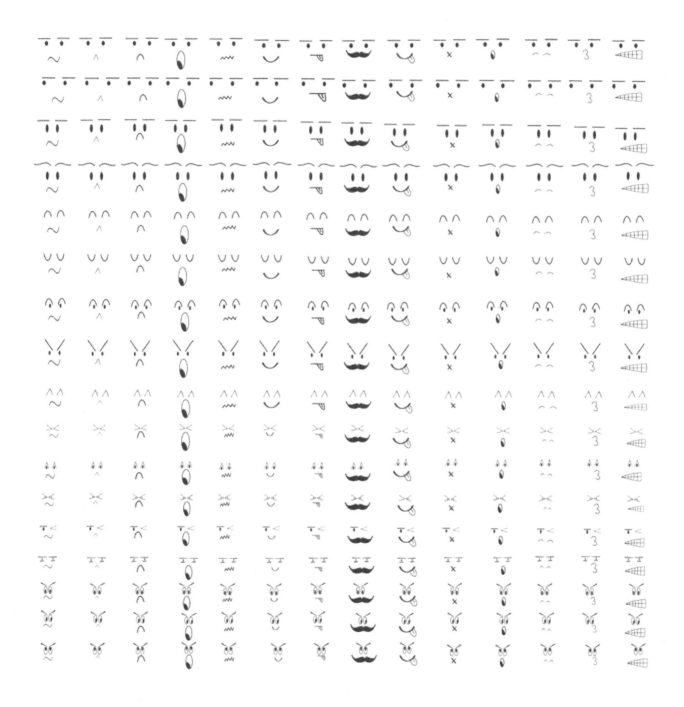

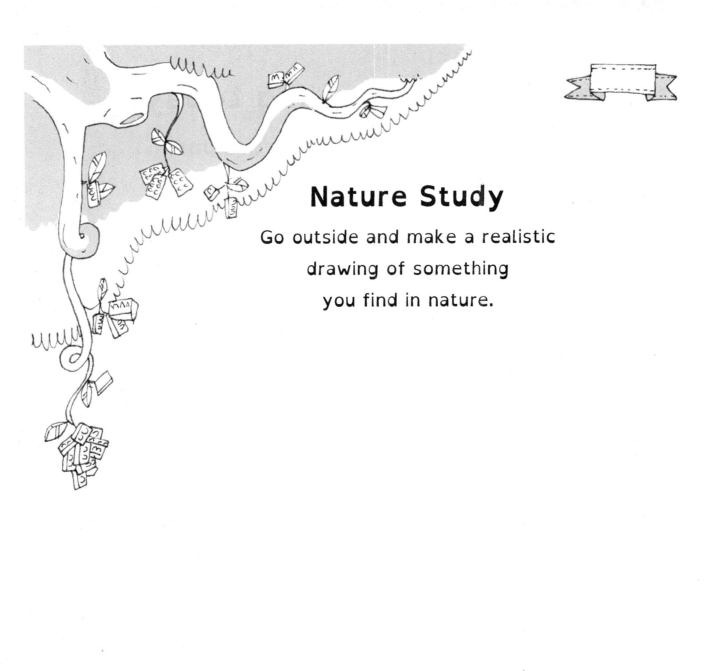

Nature Study

Go outside and make a realistic drawing of something you find in nature.

Reading Time - 1 Hour (Set a timer)

Choose Four Books - Read from each book for 15 minutes.

Copy important words or pictures from each book here:

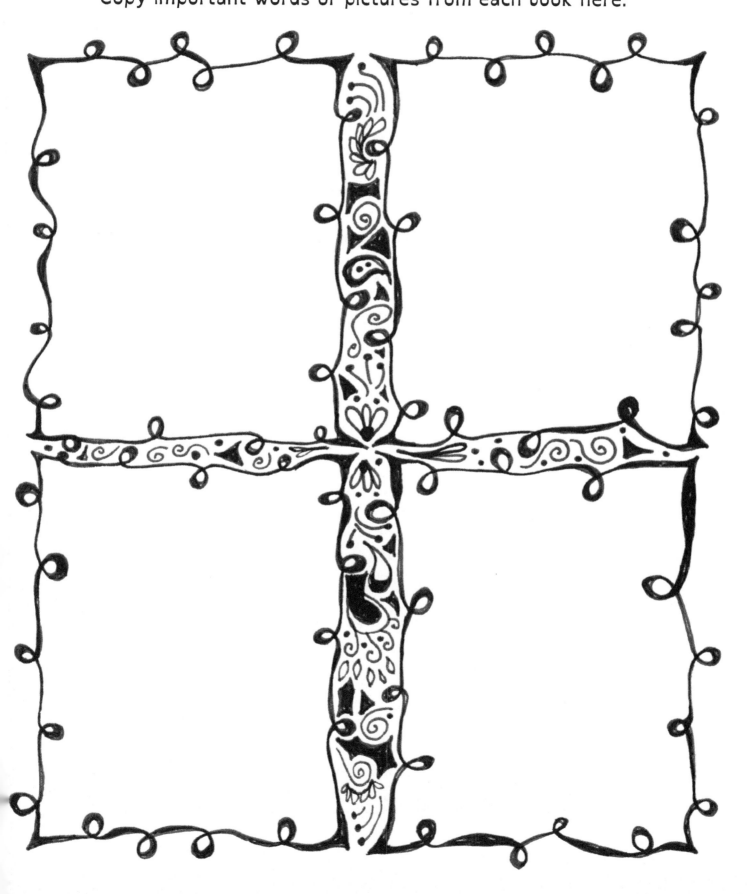

Write Today's Date:_____

Color the picture and write a story about it.

Animal Quiz

How much do you know about this animal?

Can you draw the animal's habitat, food and enemies?

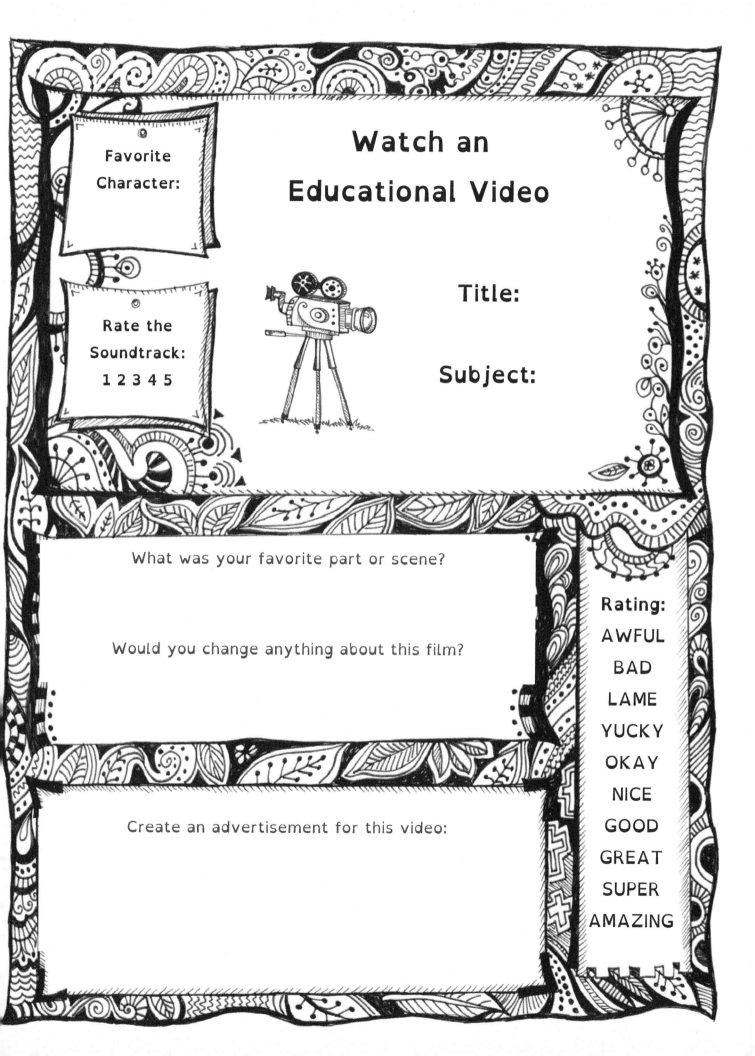

Use THIS PAGE for Math Practice
Or be creative and design something, like a house! You could make graphs, maps or geometric designs with this graph paper.

World News Today!

Talk to your parents about current events.
Look at a newspaper, news broadcast or website.
Tell the news stories with words and pictures.

WHO:

WHAT:

WHEN:

WHERE:

WHY:

Book Time

Find an interesting sentence in one of your books and copy it. Draw a picture to go with the words.

TITLE: _____

Page Number: _____

Thinking Time!

Can you complete the puzzle?

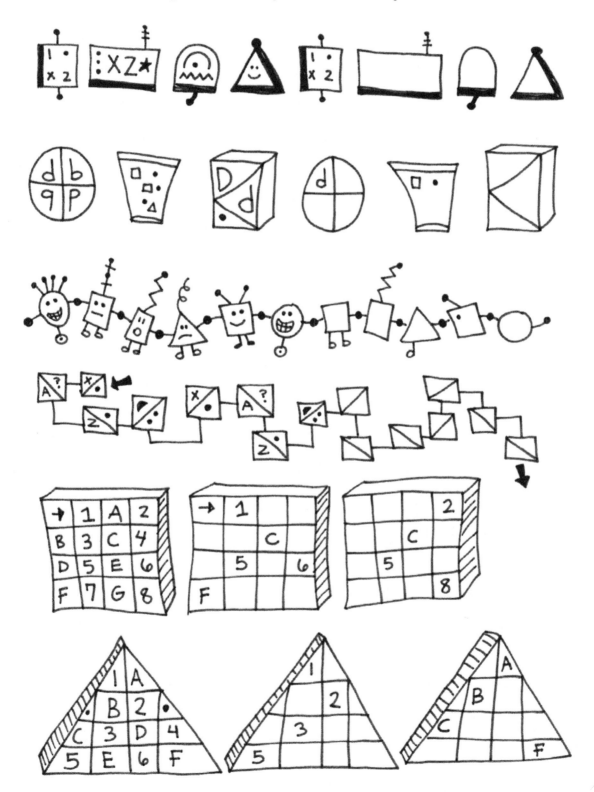

Today's Date:_____

Copy a Verse or Quote

My Plans:

To-Do List

LETTER DOODLES

Practice working with your colored pencils and learn to draw amazing letters too!

Object Lesson

Look at this picture.
List four things that you
can do with this object.

1. _____
2. _____
3. _____
4. _____

How are you feeling today?
Color the facial expressions that match your mood.

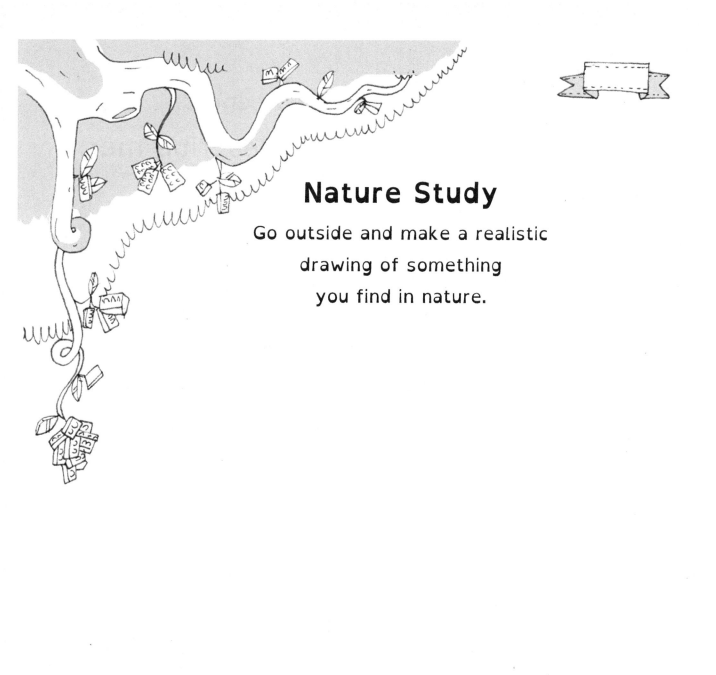

Nature Study

Go outside and make a realistic drawing of something you find in nature.

Color me with colored pencils.

Write just one word to describe me:

_____

Reading Time - 1 Hour (Set a timer)

Choose Four Books - Read from each book for 15 minutes.

Copy important words or pictures from each book here:

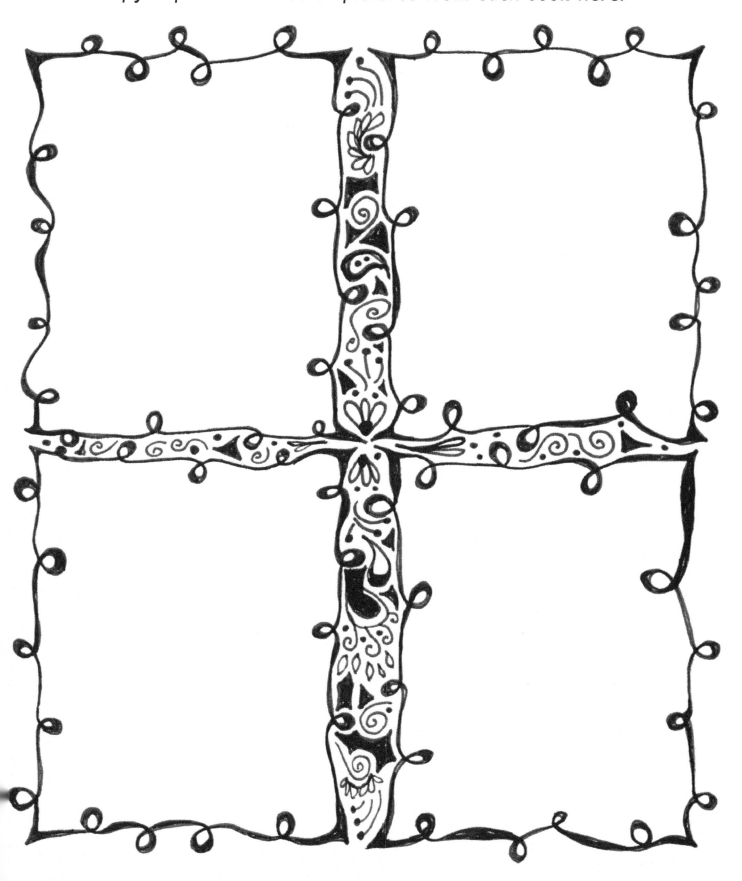

Spelling Time

Find 20 Words with 5 letters each.
Look in your books for words.
Write the words here:

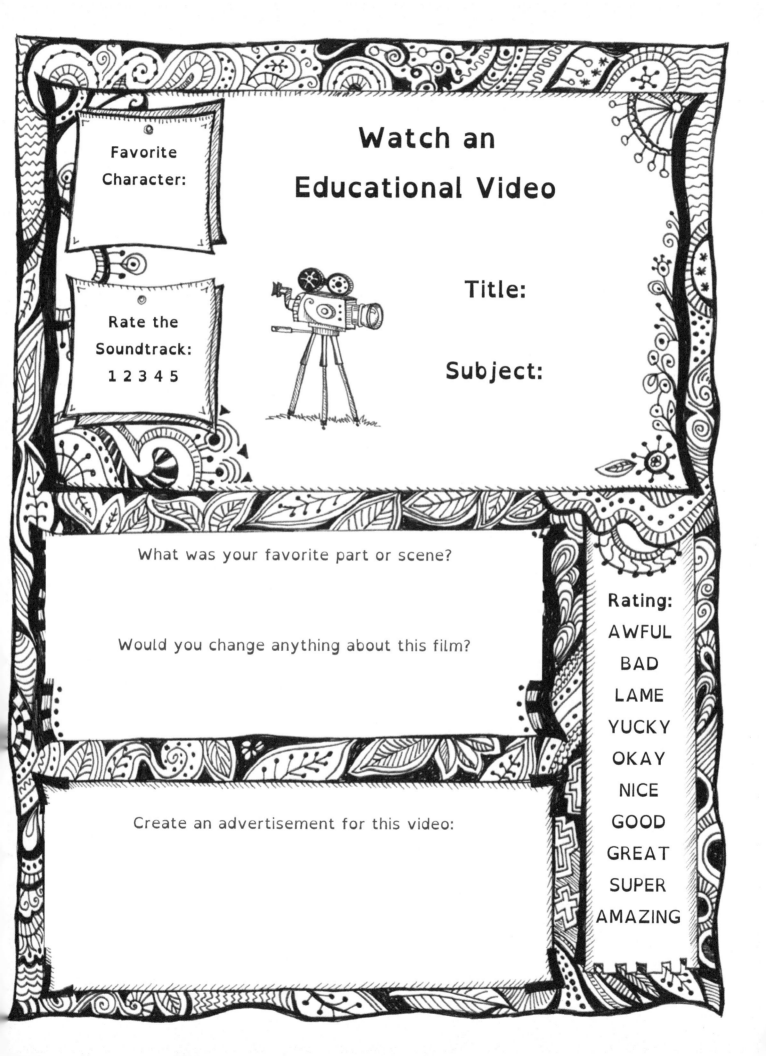

Use THIS PAGE for Math Practice

Or be creative and design something, like a house! You could make graphs, maps or geometric designs with this graph paper.

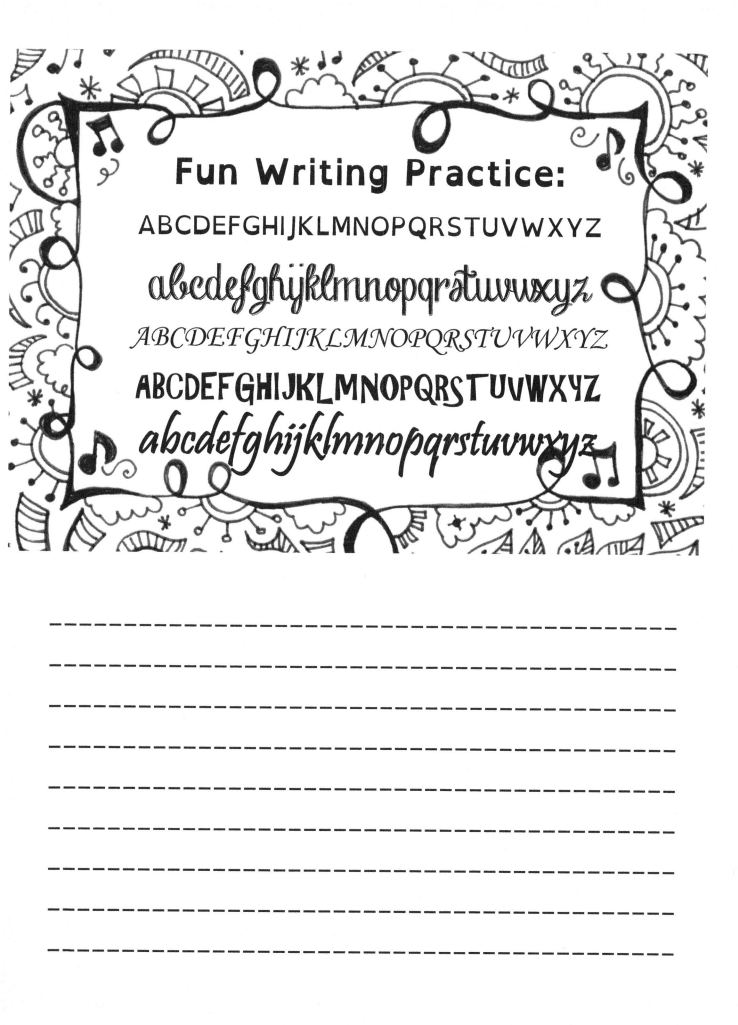

Book Time

Find an interesting sentence in one of your books and copy it. Draw a picture to go with the words.

TITLE: _____

Page Number: _____

Thinking Time!

Can you complete the puzzle?

☺ = 0	👤 = 1	🌸 = 2	☾ = 3	★ = 4
☀ = 5	🌳 = 6	☕ = 7	🧁 = 8	⬜ = 9

Write Today's Date: _____

Color the picture and write a story about it.

Today's Date:_____

Copy a Verse or Quote

My Plans:

To-Do List

LETTER DOODLES

Practice working with your colored pencils and learn to draw amazing letters too!

Object Lesson

Look at this picture.
List four things that you
can do with this object.

1. _____
2. _____
3. _____
4. _____

Color me with colored pencils.
Write just one word to describe me:

_____

How are you feeling today?
Color the facial expression

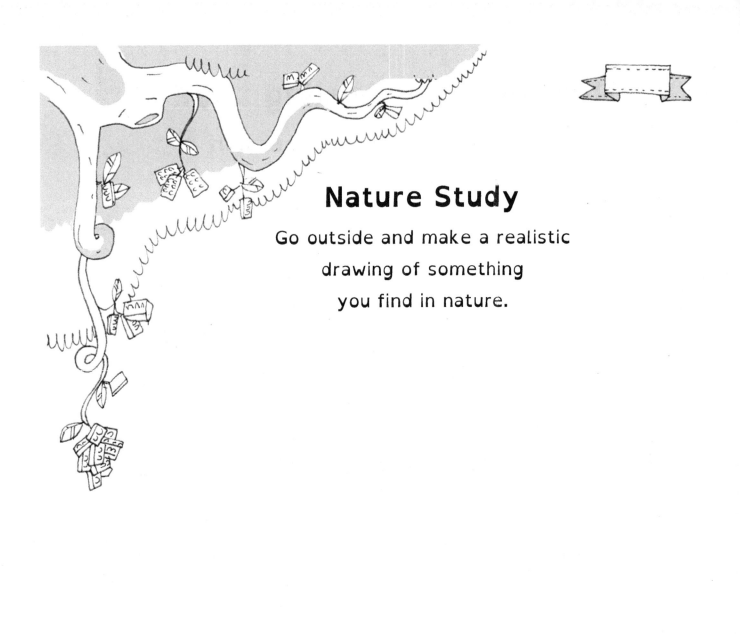

Nature Study

Go outside and make a realistic drawing of something you find in nature.

Reading Time - 1 Hour (Set a timer)

Choose Four Books - Read from each book for 15 minutes.

Copy important words or pictures from each book here:

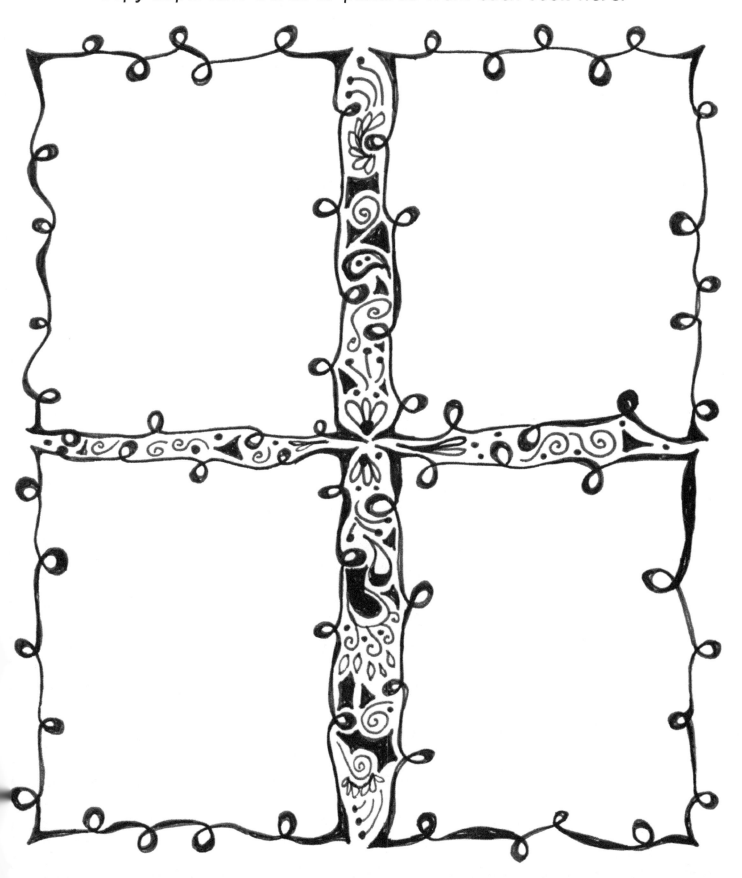

Spelling Time

Find 20 Words with **4** letters each.
Look in your books for words.
Write the words here:

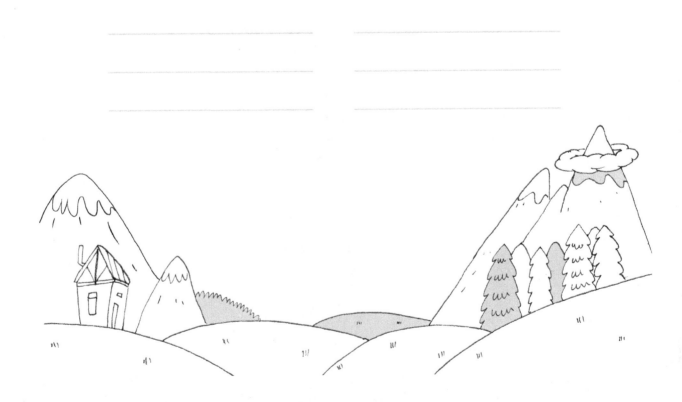

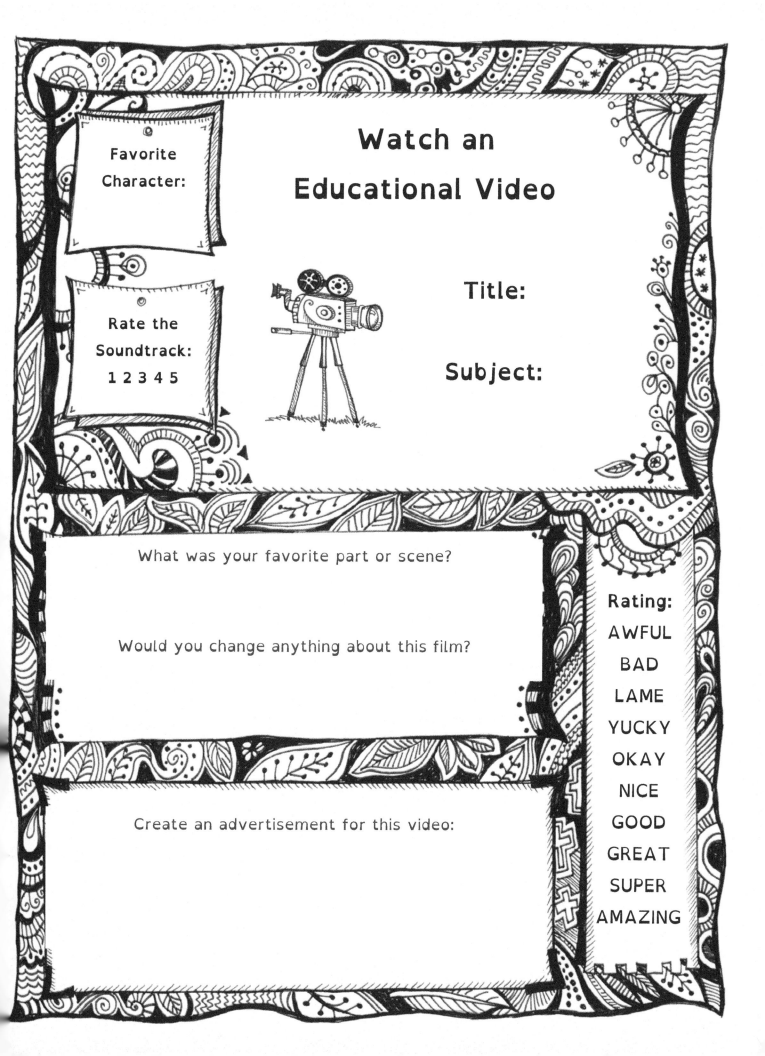

Use THIS PAGE for Math Practice
Or be creative and design something, like a house! You could make graphs, maps or geometric designs with this graph paper.

Listening Time

Listen to an audio book or classical music or ask someone to read a story to you while you color and draw on the next page.

What are you listening to?

_____

Thinking Time!

Can you complete the puzzle?

Today's Date:_____

Copy a Verse or Quote

My Plans:

To-Do List

LETTER DOODLES

Practice working with your colored pencils and learn to draw amazing letters too!

Color me with colored pencils.
Write just one word to describe me:

_____

Write Today's Date:_____

Color the picture and write a story about it.

Object Lesson

Look at this picture.
List four things that you
can do with this object.

1. _____
2. _____
3. _____
4. _____

How are you feeling today?//
Color the facial expressions that match your mood.

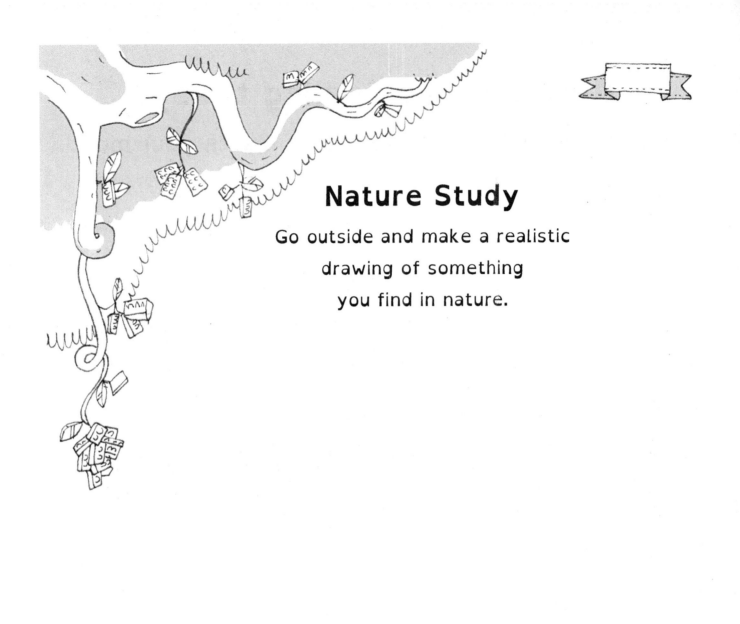

Nature Study

Go outside and make a realistic drawing of something you find in nature.

Reading Time - 1 Hour (Set a timer)

Choose Four Books - Read from each book for 15 minutes.

Copy important words or pictures from each book here:

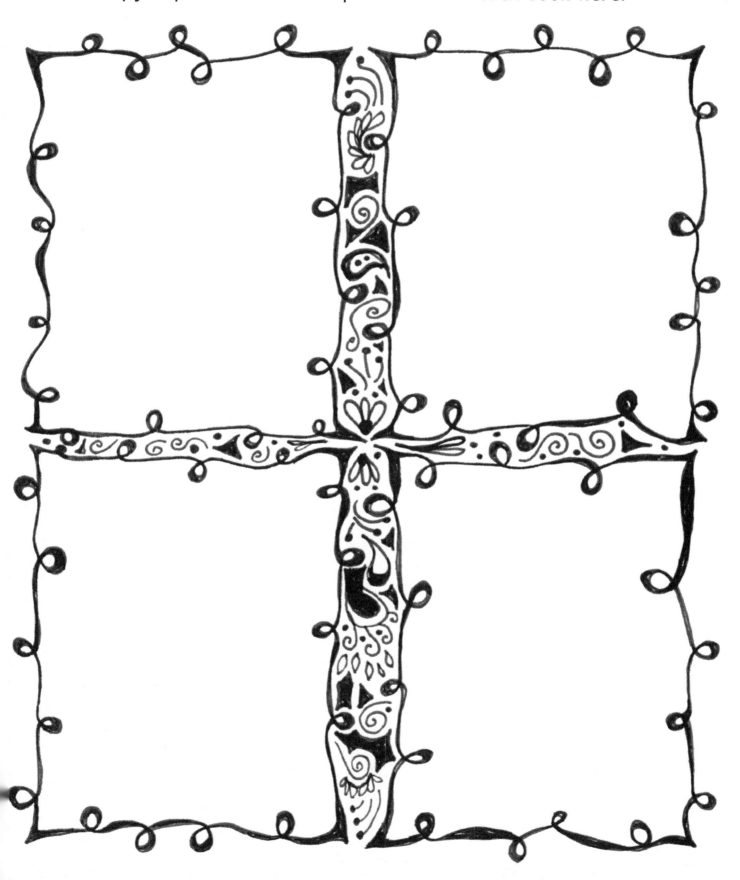

Spelling Time

Find 20 Words with 3 letters each.
Look in your books for words.
Write the words here:

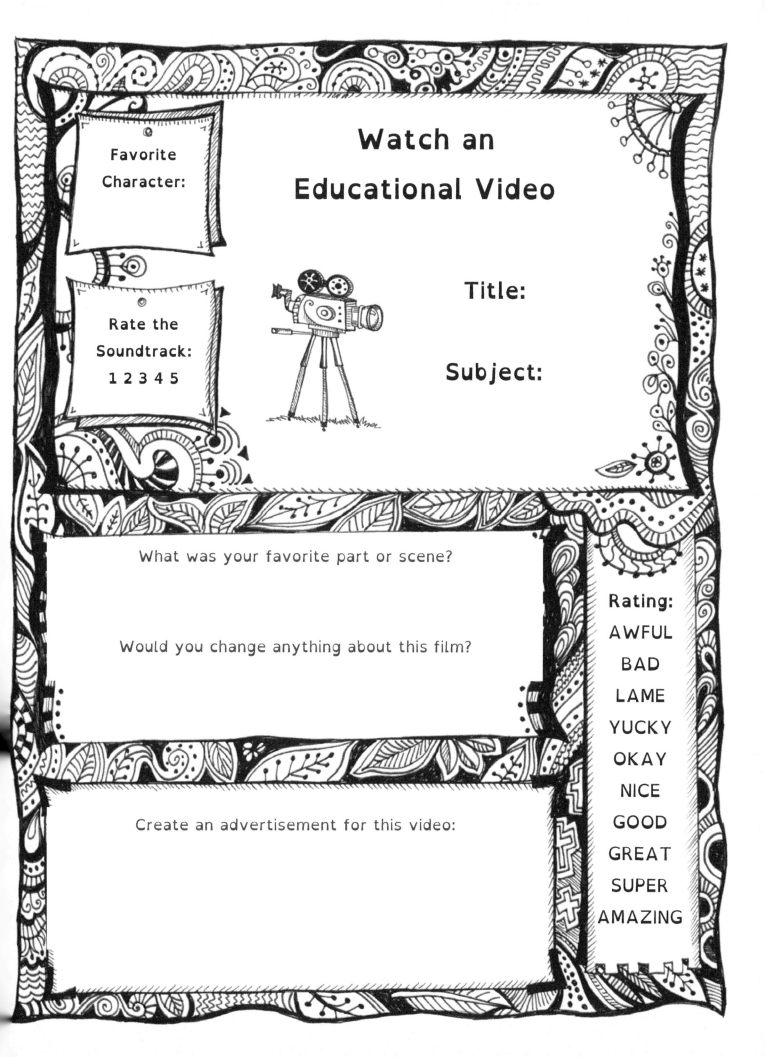

Use THIS PAGE for Math Practice
Or be creative and design something, like a house! You could make graphs, maps or geometric designs with this graph paper.

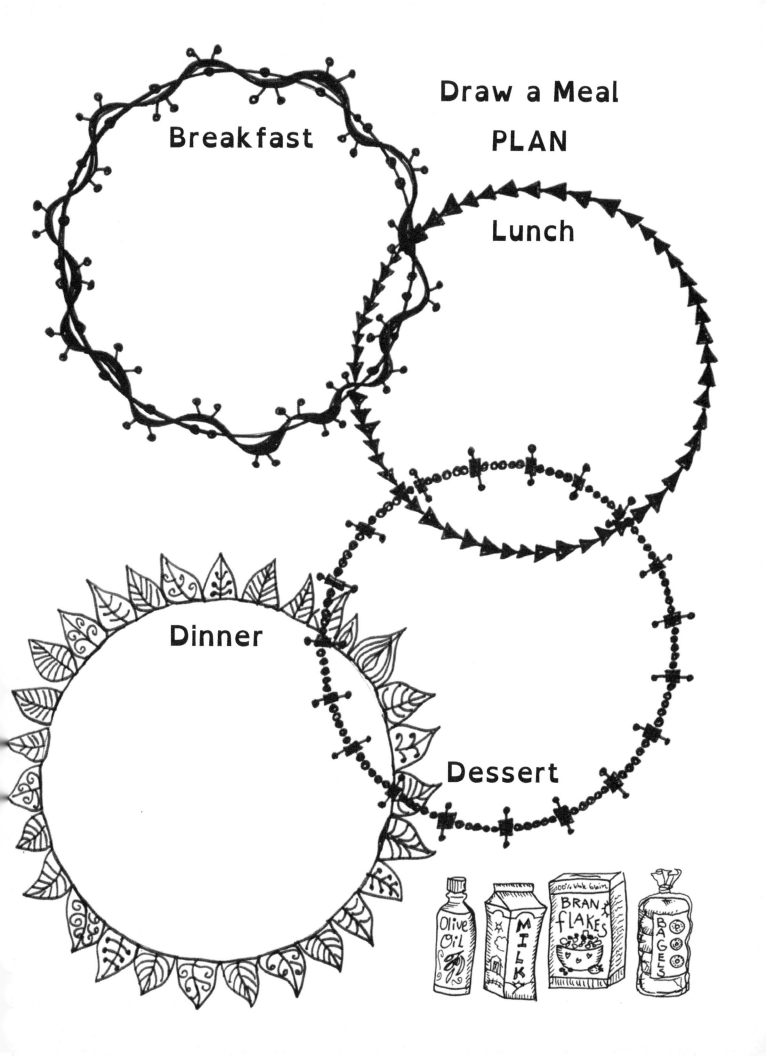

Book Time

Find an interesting sentence in one of your books and copy it. Draw a picture to go with the words.

TITLE: _____

Page Number: _____

Thinking Time!

Can you complete the puzzle?

Color me with colored pencils.
Write just one word to describe me:

_____

Today's Date:_____

LETTER DOODLES

Practice working with your colored pencils and learn to draw amazing letters too!

Object Lesson

Look at this picture.
List four things that you
can do with this object.

1. _____
2. _____
3. _____
4. _____

How are you feeling today?
Circle all the facial expressions that best depict your moods today.

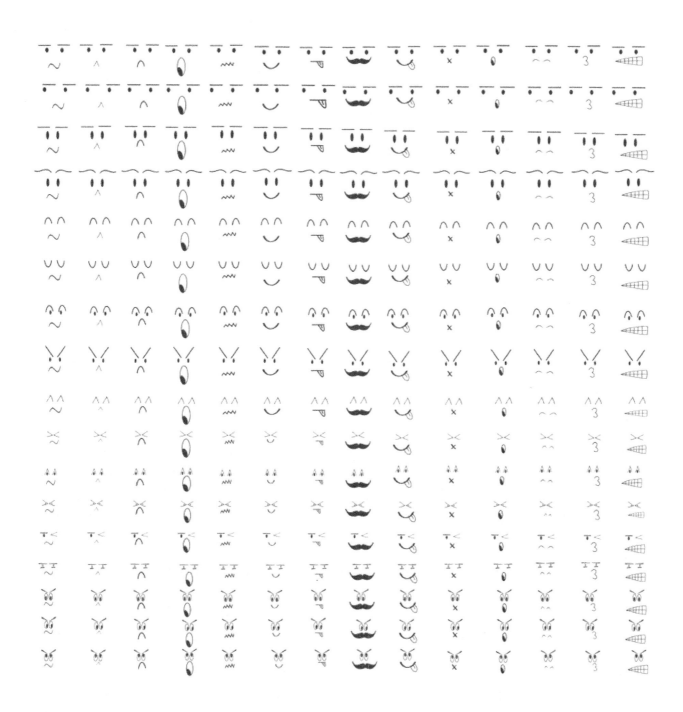

Write Today's Date:_____

Color the picture and write a story about it.

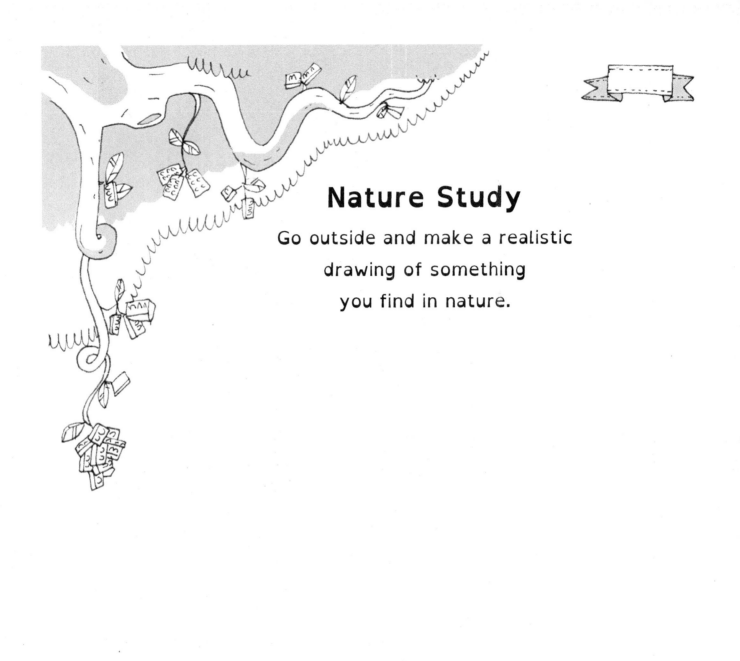

Nature Study

Go outside and make a realistic drawing of something you find in nature.

Reading Time - 1 Hour (Set a timer)
Choose Four Books - Read from each book for 15 minutes.
Copy important words or pictures from each book here:

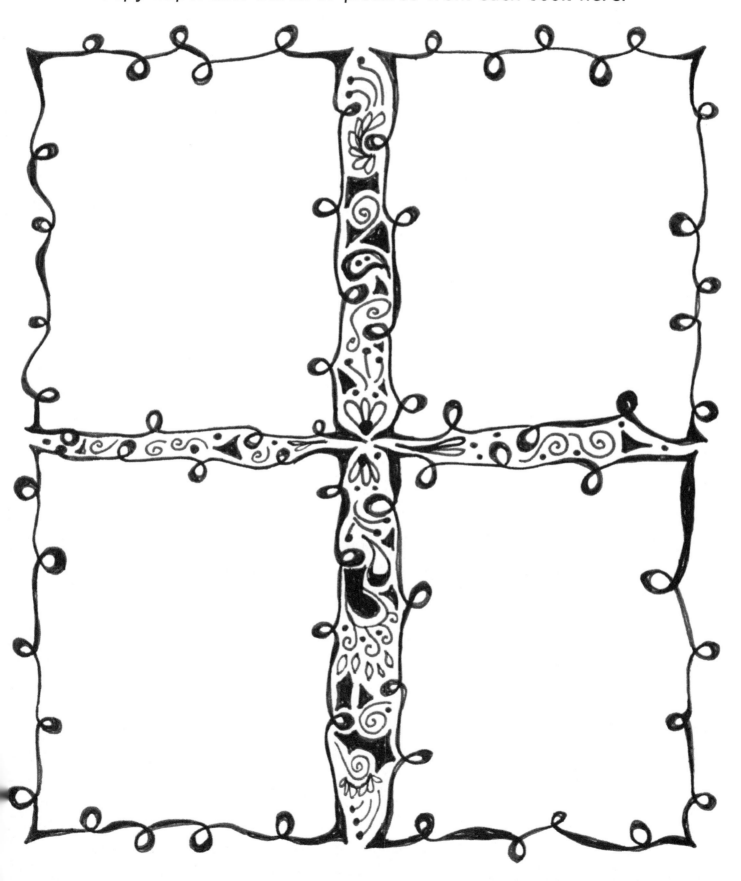

Spelling Time

Find 20 Words with **4** letters each.
Look in your books for words.
Write the words here:

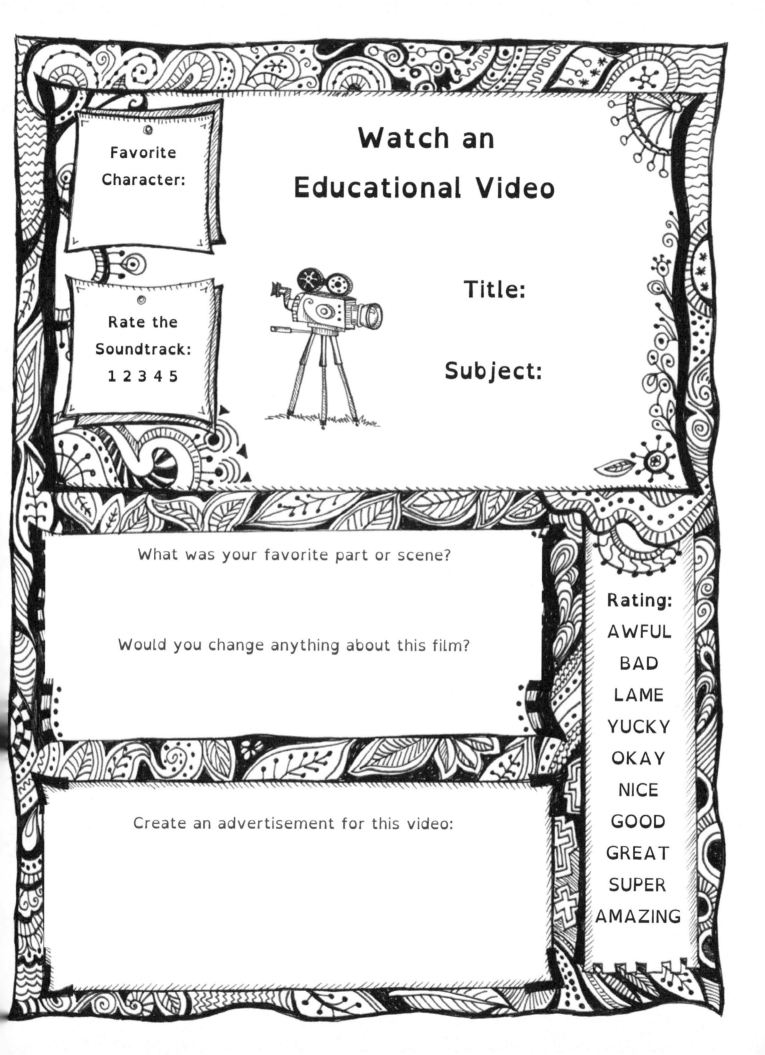

Use THIS PAGE for Math Practice
Or be creative and design something, like a house! You could make graphs, maps or geometric designs with this graph paper.

Book Time

Find an interesting sentence in one of your books and copy it. Draw a picture to go with the words.

TITLE:_____

Page Number:_____

Thinking Time!

Can you complete the puzzle?

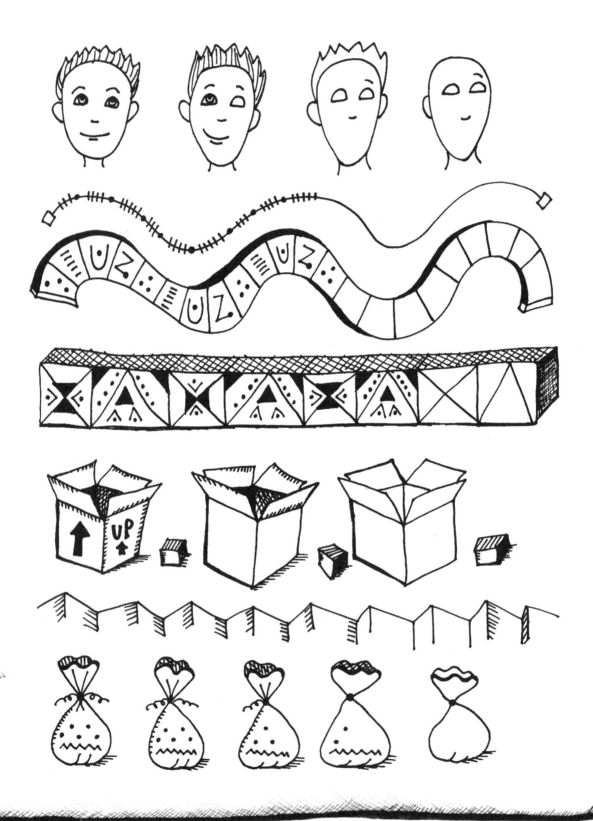

Color me with colored pencils.

Write just one word to describe me:

_____

Today's Date:_____

Copy a Verse or Quote

_____
_____
_____
_____
_____

My Plans:

_____
_____
_____
_____

To-Do List

_____
_____
_____
_____
_____
_____

LETTER DOODLES

Practice working with your colored pencils and learn to draw amazing letters too!

Object Lesson

Look at this picture.
List four things that you
can do with this object.

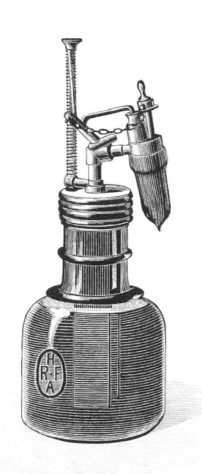

1. _____
2. _____
3. _____
4. _____

How are you feeling today?
Color the facial expressions that match your mood.

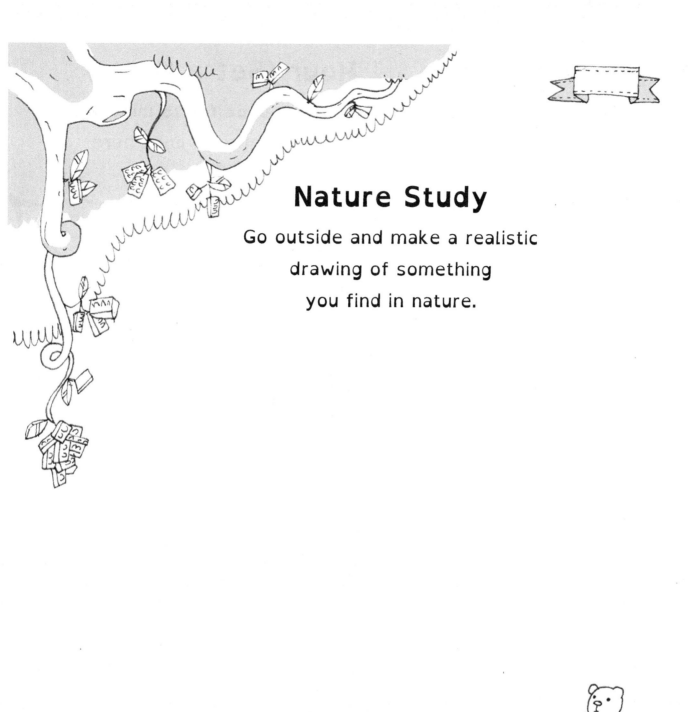

Nature Study

Go outside and make a realistic drawing of something you find in nature.

Reading Time - 1 Hour (Set a timer)

Choose Four Books - Read from each book for 15 minutes.

Copy important words or pictures from each book here:

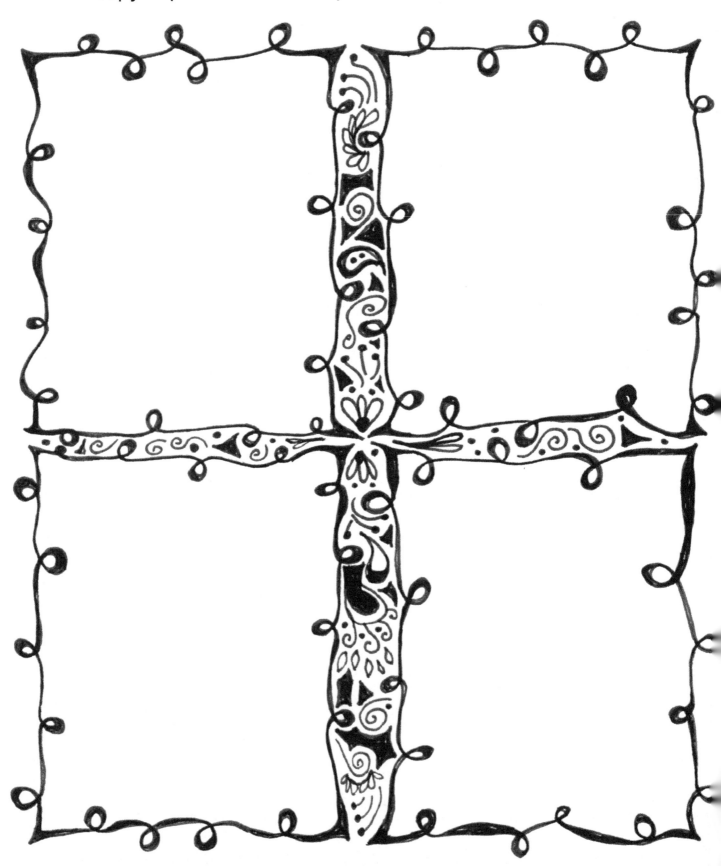

Spelling Time

Find 20 Words with 5 letters each.
Look in your books for words.
Write the words here:

Write Today's Date:_____

Color the picture and write a story about it.

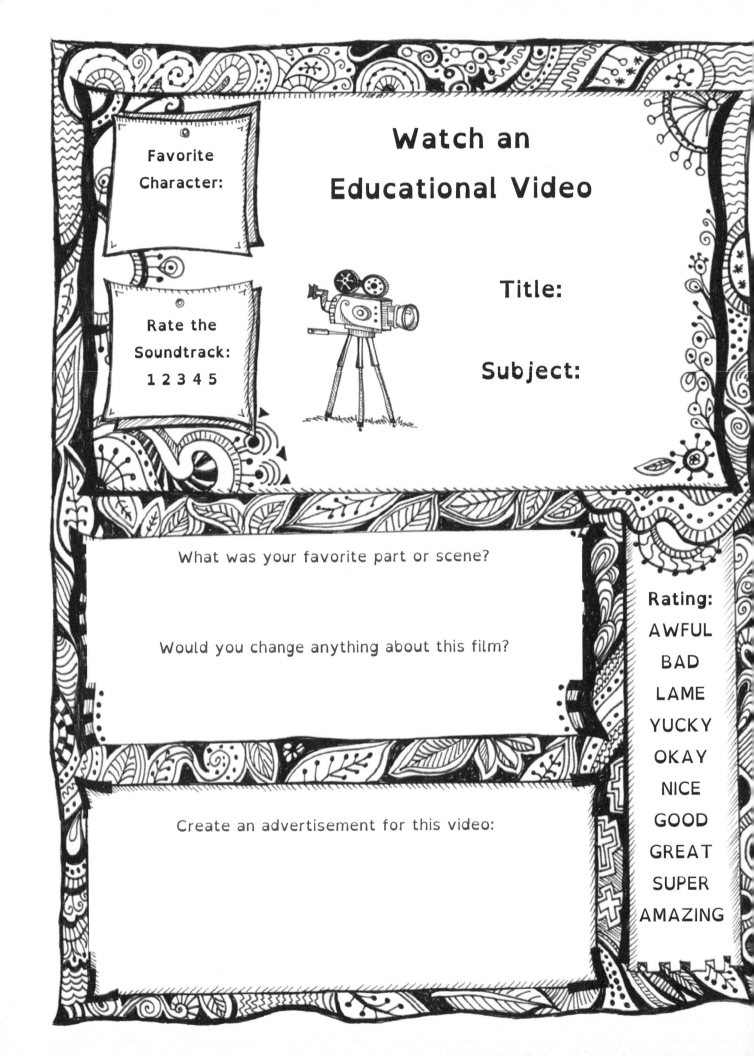

Use THIS PAGE for Math Practice
Or be creative and design something, like a house! You could make graphs, maps or geometric designs with this graph paper.

Book Time

Find an interesting sentence in one of your books and copy it. Draw a picture to go with the words.

TITLE:_____

Page Number:_____

Today's Date:_____

Copy a Verse or Quote

My Plans:

To-Do List

LETTER DOODLES

Practice working with your colored pencils and learn to draw amazing letters too!

Object Lesson

Look at this picture.
List four things that you
can do with this object.

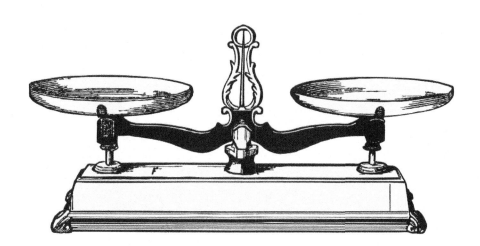

1. _____
2. _____
3. _____
4. _____

Color me with colored pencils.
Write just one word to describe me:

_____

How are you feeling today?
Color the facial expressions that match your mood.

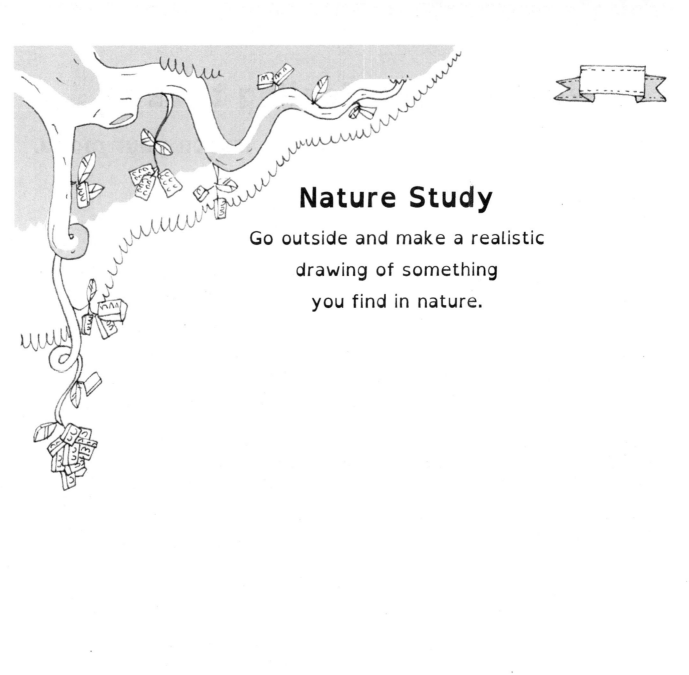

Nature Study

Go outside and make a realistic drawing of something you find in nature.

Reading Time - 1 Hour (Set a timer)

Choose Four Books - Read from each book for 15 minutes.

Copy important words or pictures from each book here:

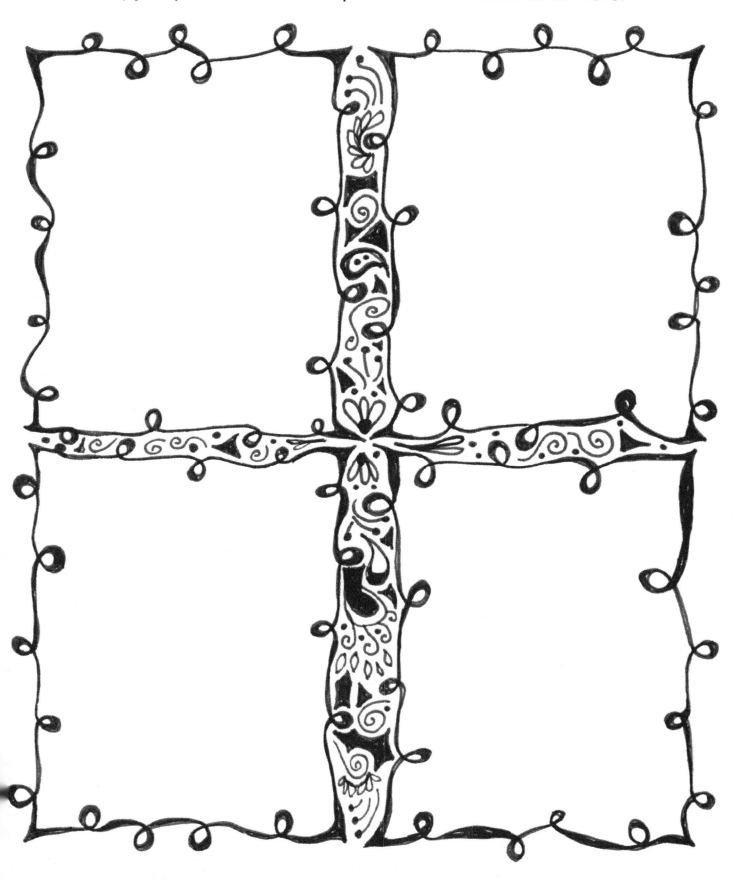

Spelling Time

Find 20 Words with 6 letters each.
Look in your books for words.
Write the words here:

Watch an Educational Video

Favorite Character:

Rate the Soundtrack:
1 2 3 4 5

Title:

Subject:

What was your favorite part or scene?

Would you change anything about this film?

Create an advertisement for this video:

Rating:
AWFUL
BAD
LAME
YUCKY
OKAY
NICE
GOOD
GREAT
SUPER
AMAZING

Use THIS PAGE for Math Practice
Or be creative and design something, like a house! You could make graphs, maps or geometric designs with this graph paper.

World News Today!

Talk to your parents about current events.
Look at a newspaper, news broadcast or website.
Tell the news stories with words and pictures.

WHO:

WHAT:

WHEN:

WHERE:

WHY:

Book Time

Find an interesting sentence in one of your books and copy it. Draw a picture to go with the words.

TITLE: _____

Page Number: _____

Thinking Time!

Can you complete the puzzle?

Today's Date:_____

Copy a Verse or Quote

_____
_____
_____
_____
_____

My Plans:
_____
_____
_____
_____

To-Do List
_____
_____
_____
_____
_____
_____

LETTER DOODLES

Practice working with your colored pencils and learn to draw amazing letters too!

Object Lesson

Look at this picture.
List four things that you
can do with this object.

1. _____
2. _____
3. _____
4. _____

Write Today's Date:_____

Color the picture and write a story about it.

How are you feeling today?
Color the facial expressions that match your mood.

Color me with colored pencils.
Write just one word to describe me:

_____

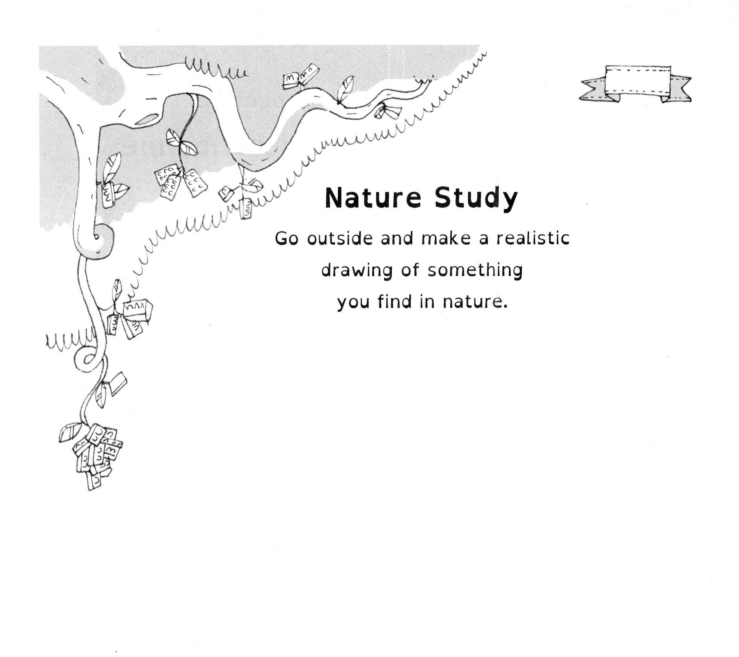

Nature Study

Go outside and make a realistic drawing of something you find in nature.

Reading Time - 1 Hour (Set a timer)

Choose Four Books - Read from each book for 15 minutes.

Copy important words or pictures from each book here:

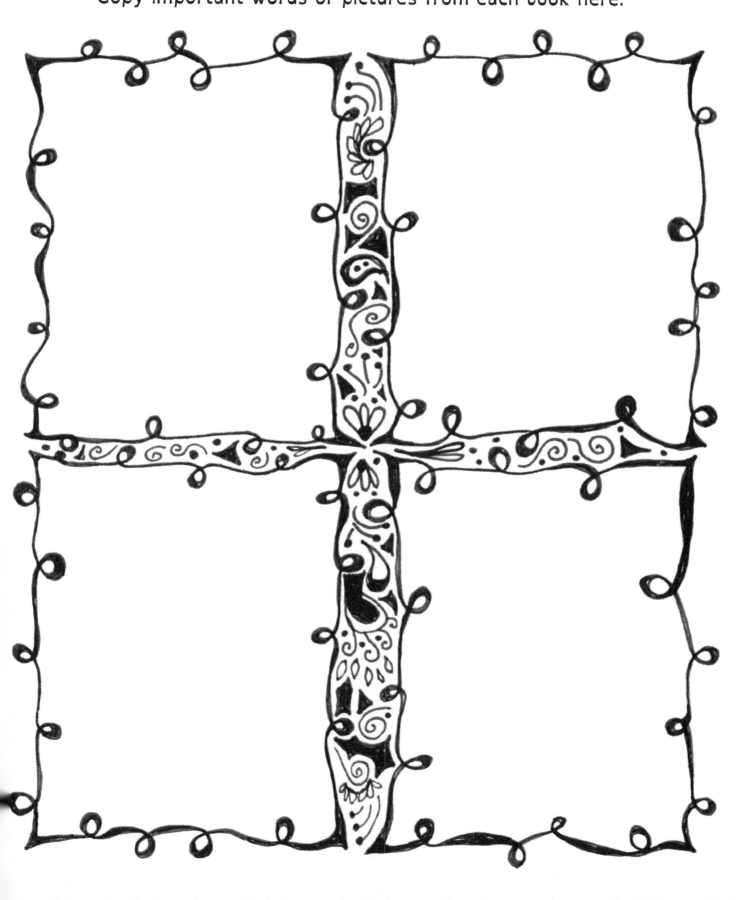

Spelling Time

Find 20 Words with 7 letters each.
Look in your books for words.
Write the words here:

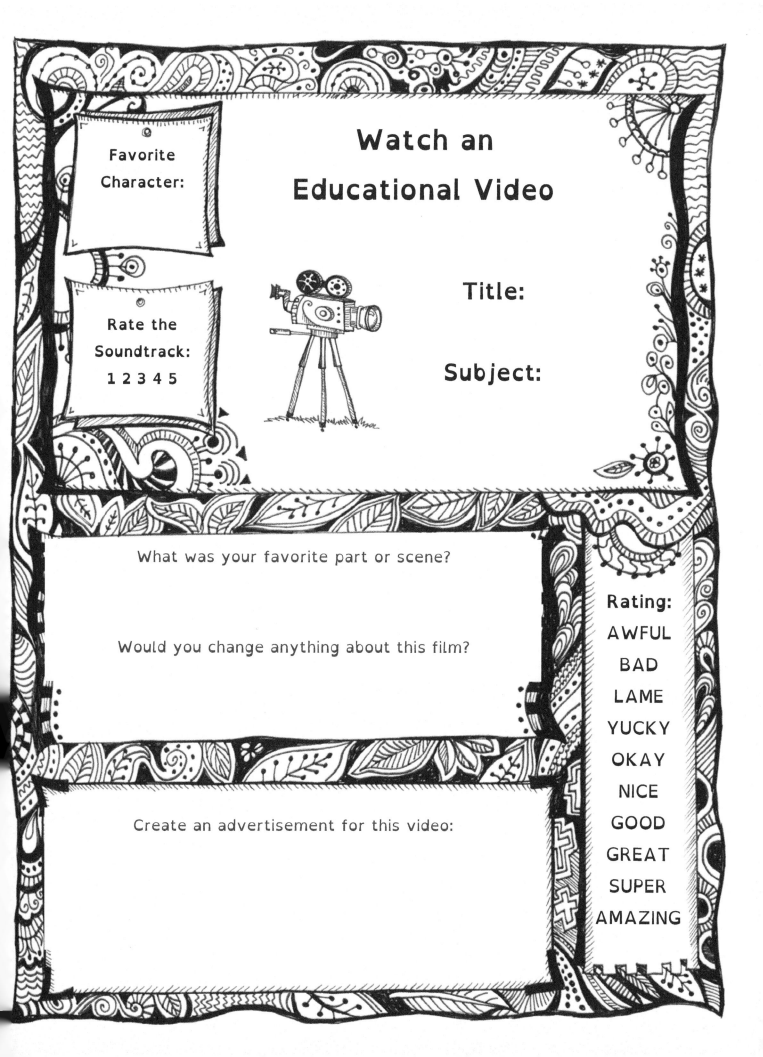

Use THIS PAGE for Math Practice

Or be creative and design something, like a house! You could make graphs, maps or geometric designs with this graph paper.

Book Time

Find an interesting sentence in one of your books and copy it. Draw a picture to go with the words.

TITLE:_____

Page Number:_____

Thinking Time!

Can you complete the puzzle?

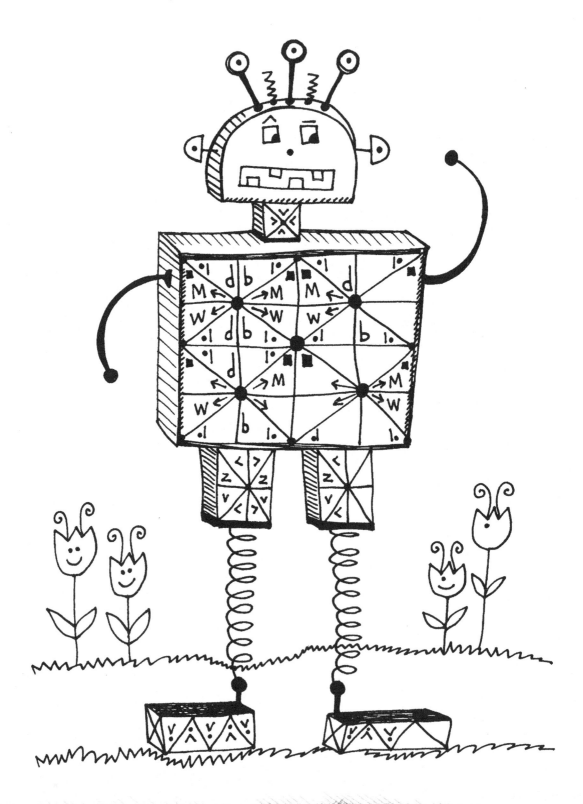

Today's Date:_____

Copy a Verse or Quote

_____
_____
_____
_____
_____

My Plans:

_____
_____
_____
_____

To-Do List

_____
_____
_____
_____
_____
_____

LETTER DOODLES

Practice working with your colored pencils and learn to draw amazing letters too!

Object Lesson

Look at this picture.
List four things that you
can do with this object.

1. _____
2. _____
3. _____
4. _____

How are you feeling today?
Color the facial expressions that match your mood.

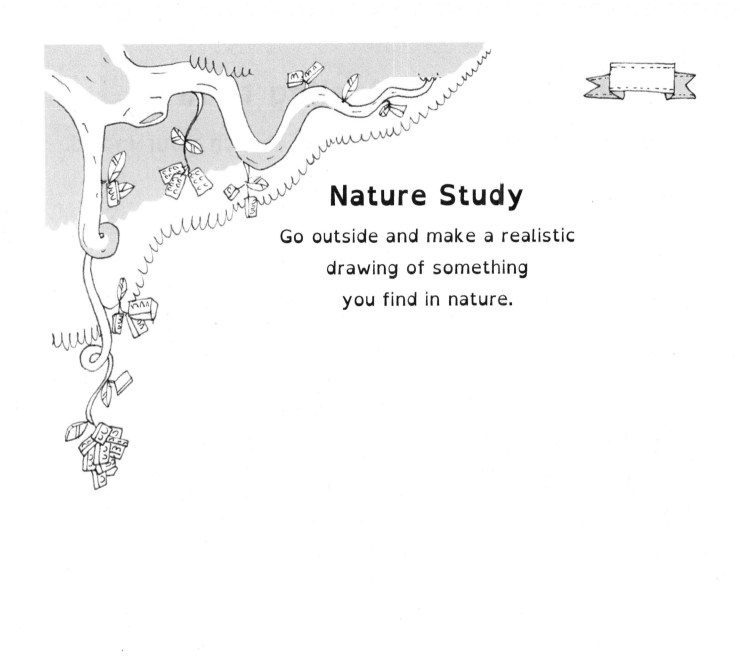

Nature Study

Go outside and make a realistic drawing of something you find in nature.

Reading Time - 1 Hour (Set a timer)

Choose Four Books - Read from each book for 15 minutes.

Copy important words or pictures from each book here:

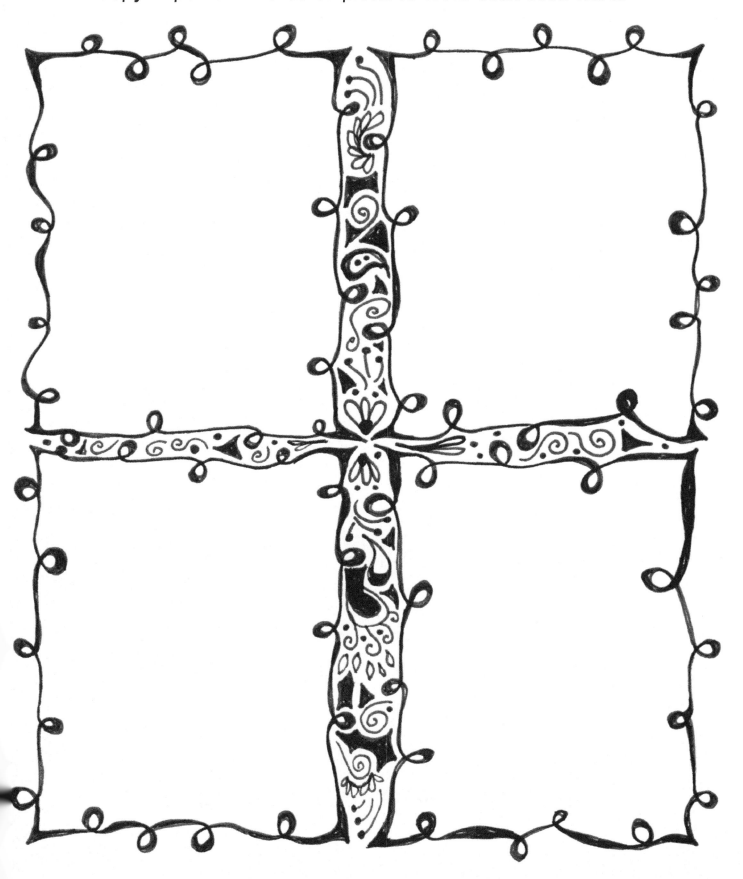

Write Today's Date: _____

Color the picture and write a story about it.

Color me with colored pencils.
Write just one word to describe me:
_____

Spelling Time

Find 20 Words with 8 letters each.
Look in your books for words.
Write the words here:

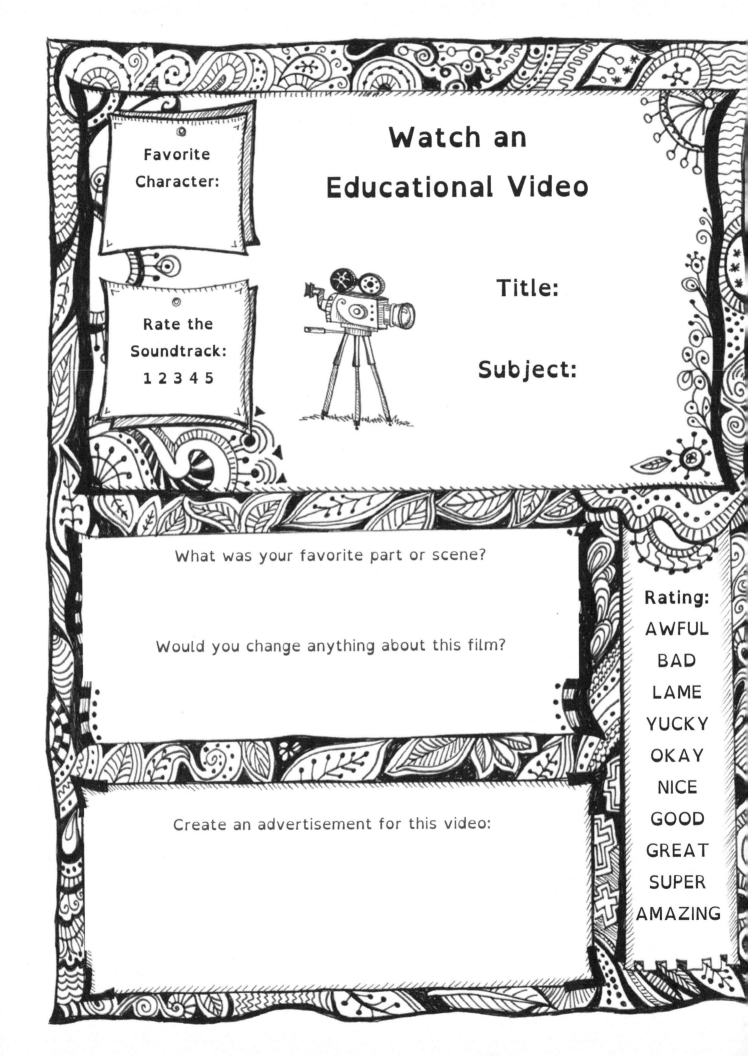

Use THIS PAGE for Math Practice

Or be creative and design something, like a house! You could make graphs, maps or geometric designs with this graph paper.

Listening Time

Listen to an audio book or classical music or ask someone to read a story to you while you color and draw on the next page.

What are you listening to?

_____

Thinking Time!

Can you complete the puzzle?

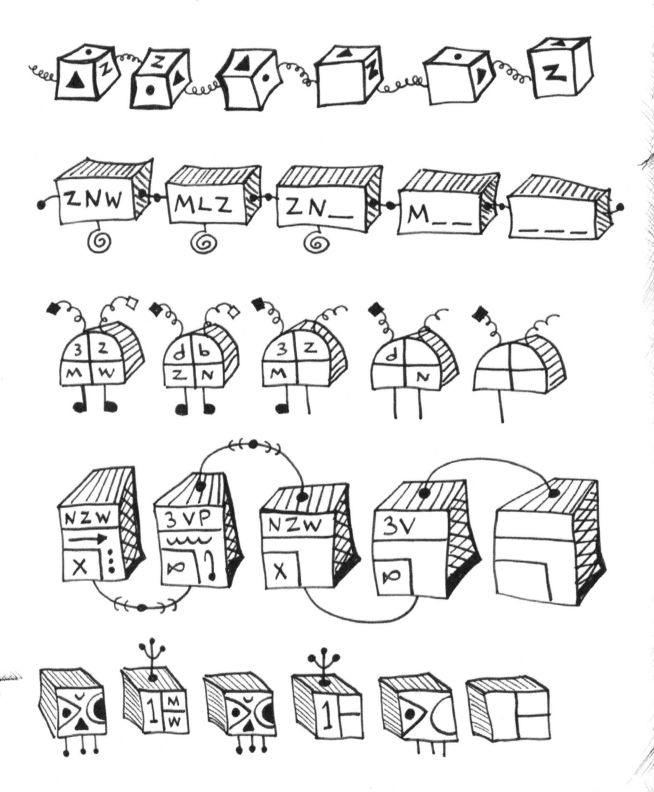

Today's Date: _____

Copy a Verse or Quote

_____
_____
_____
_____
_____

My Plans:

_____
_____
_____
_____

To-Do List

_____
_____
_____
_____
_____
_____

LETTER DOODLES

Practice working with your colored pencils and learn to draw amazing letters too!

Object Lesson

Look at this picture.
List four things that you
can do with this object.

1. _____
2. _____
3. _____
4. _____

How are you feeling today?
Circle all the facial expressions that best depict your moods today.

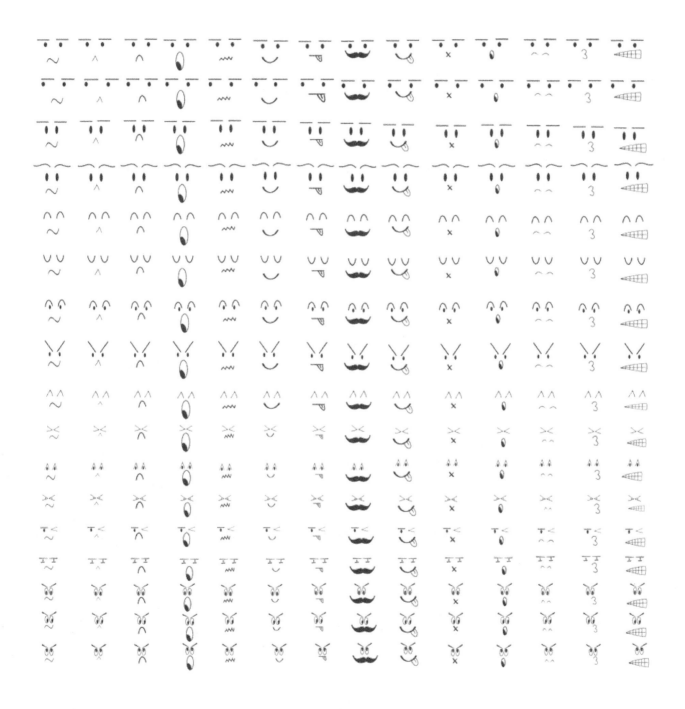

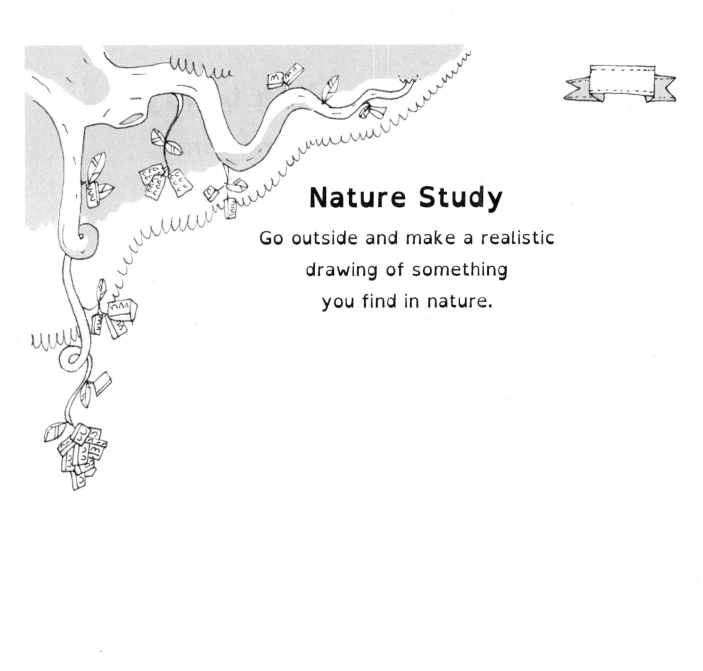

Nature Study

Go outside and make a realistic drawing of something you find in nature.

Reading Time - 1 Hour (Set a timer)

Choose Four Books - Read from each book for 15 minutes.

Copy important words or pictures from each book here:

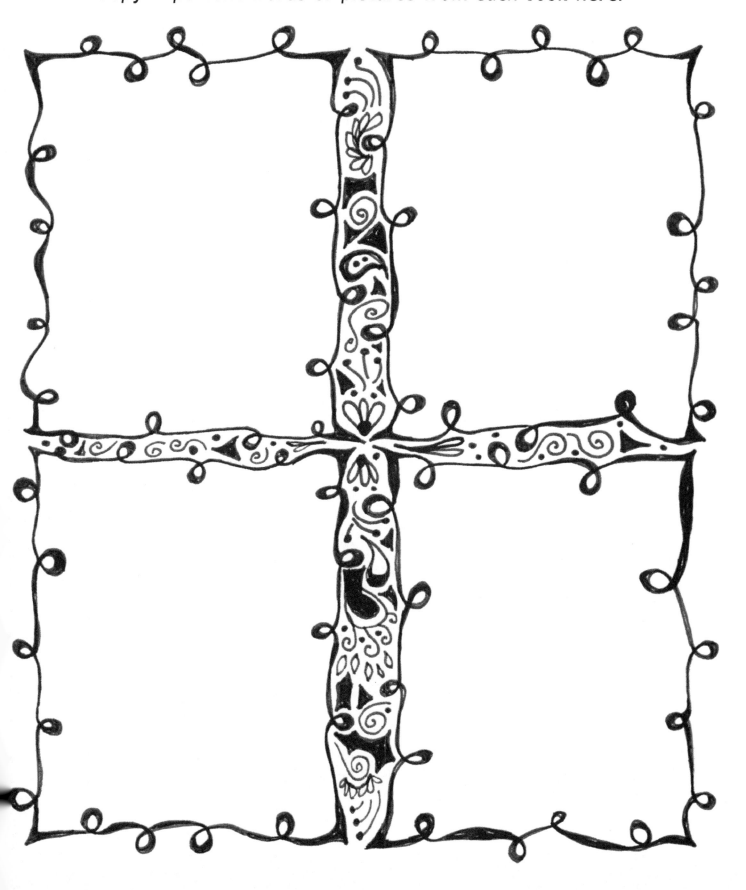

Spelling Time

Find 20 Words with 9 letters each.
Look in your books for words.
Write the words here:

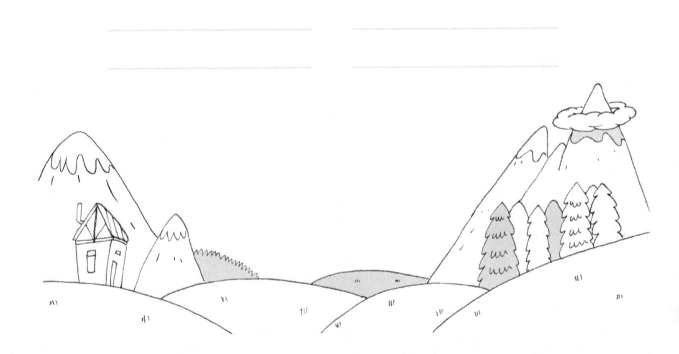

Color me with colored pencils.

Write just one word to describe me:

_____

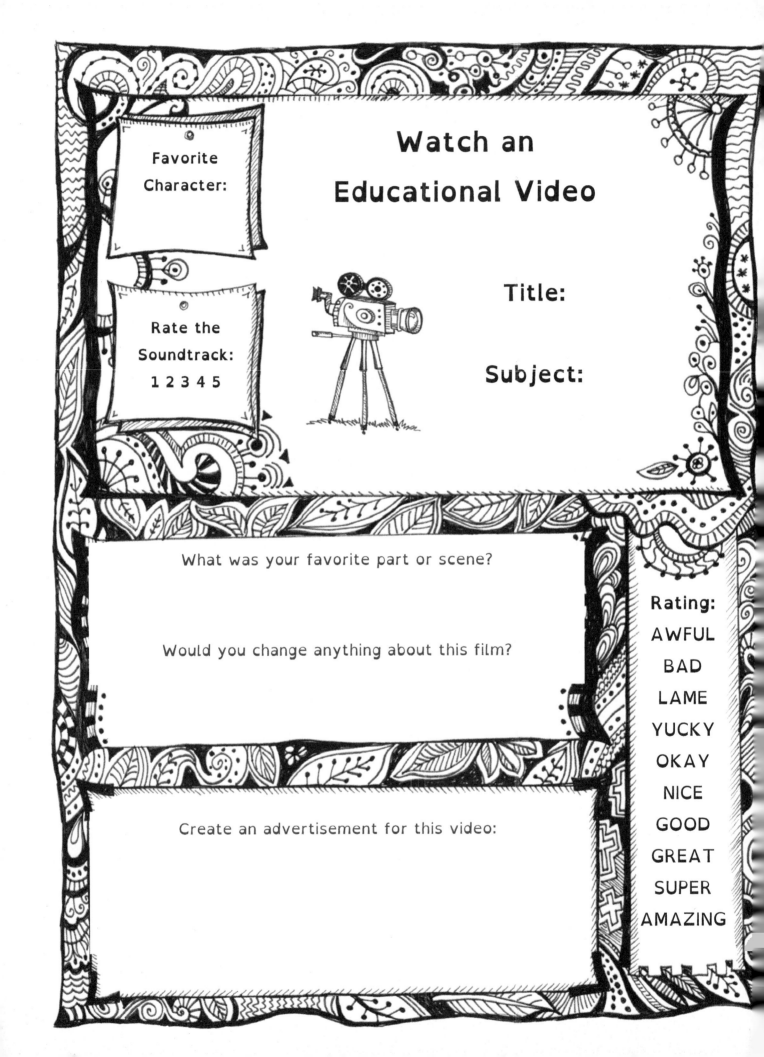

Use THIS PAGE for Math Practice

Or be creative and design something, like a house! You could make graphs, maps or geometric designs with this graph paper.

World News Today!

Talk to your parents about current events.
Look at a newspaper, news broadcast or website.
Tell the news stories with words and pictures.

WHO:

WHAT:

WHEN:

WHERE:

WHY:

Book Time

Find an interesting sentence in one of your books and copy it. Draw a picture to go with the words.

TITLE:_____

Page Number:_____

Write Today's Date: _____

Color the picture and write a story about it.

Thinking Time!

Can you complete the puzzle?

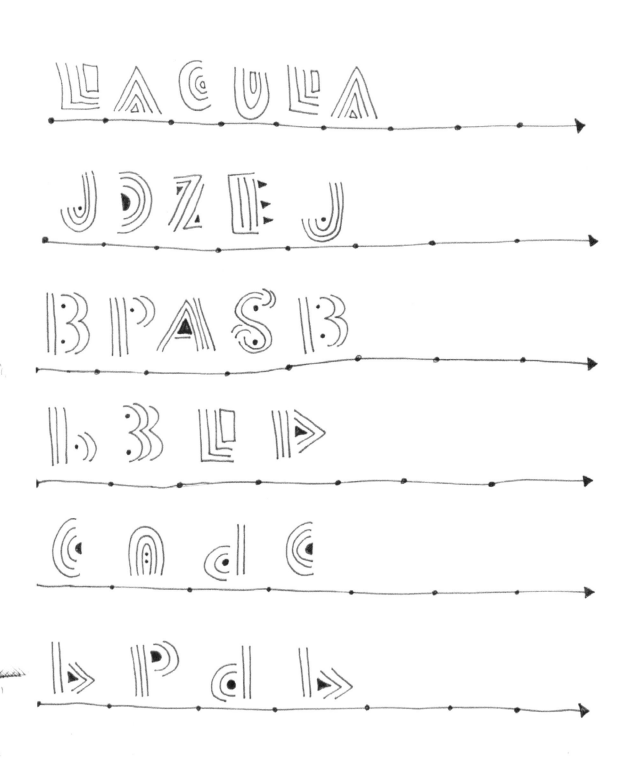

Today's Date:_____

Copy a Verse or Quote

_____
_____
_____
_____
_____

My Plans:

_____
_____
_____
_____

To-Do List

_____
_____
_____
_____
_____
_____

LETTER DOODLES

Practice working with your colored pencils and learn to draw amazing letters too!

Object Lesson

Look at this picture.
List four things that you
can do with this object.

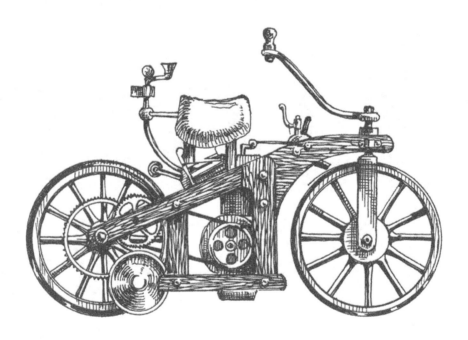

1._____
2._____
3._____
4._____

How are you feeling today?
Color the facial expressions that match your mood.

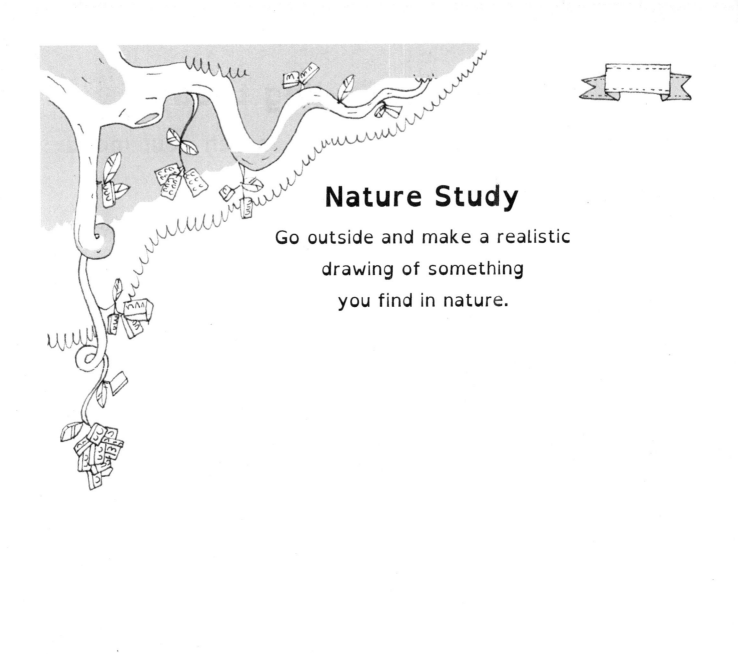

Nature Study

Go outside and make a realistic drawing of something you find in nature.

Reading Time - 1 Hour (Set a timer)

Choose Four Books - Read from each book for 15 minutes.

Copy important words or pictures from each book here:

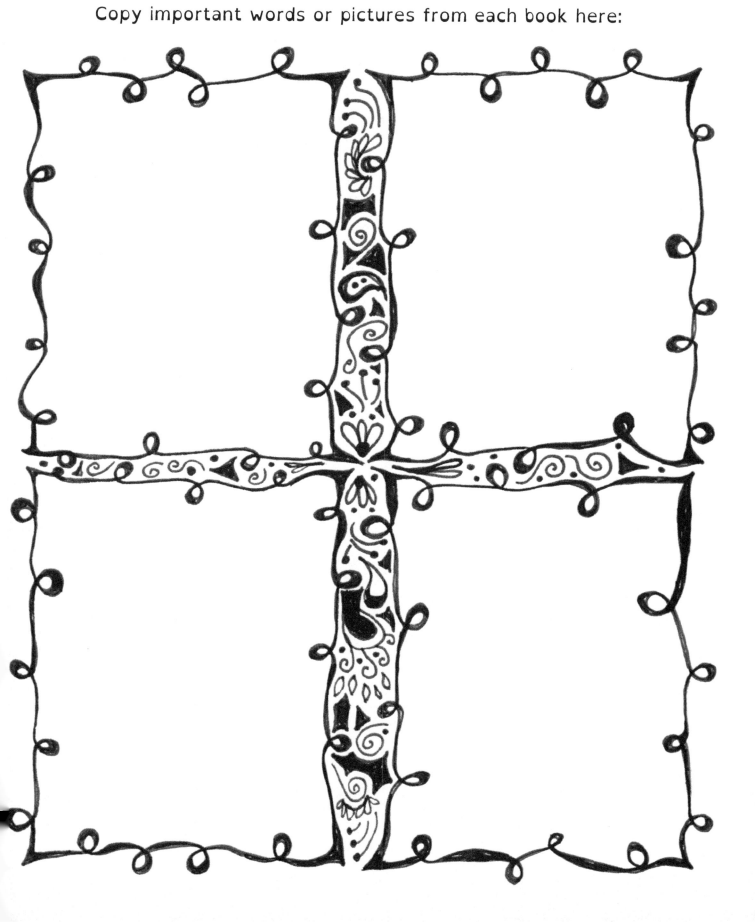

Spelling Time

Find 20 Words with **8** letters each.
Look in your books for words.
Write the words here:

Reading Time - 1 Hour (Set a timer)

Choose Four Books - Read from each book for 15 minutes.

Copy important words or pictures from each book here:

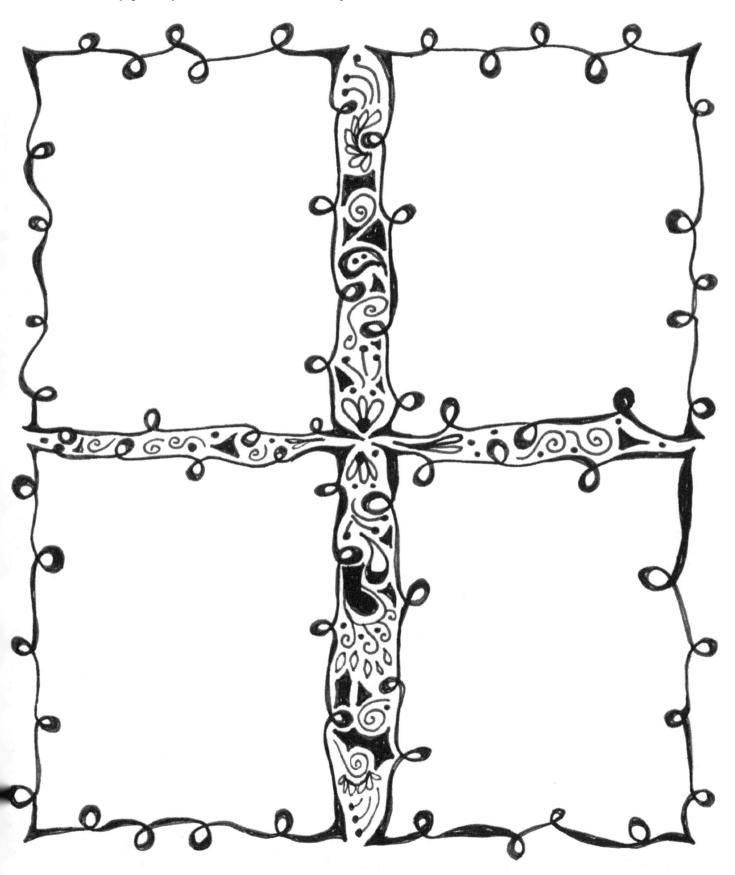

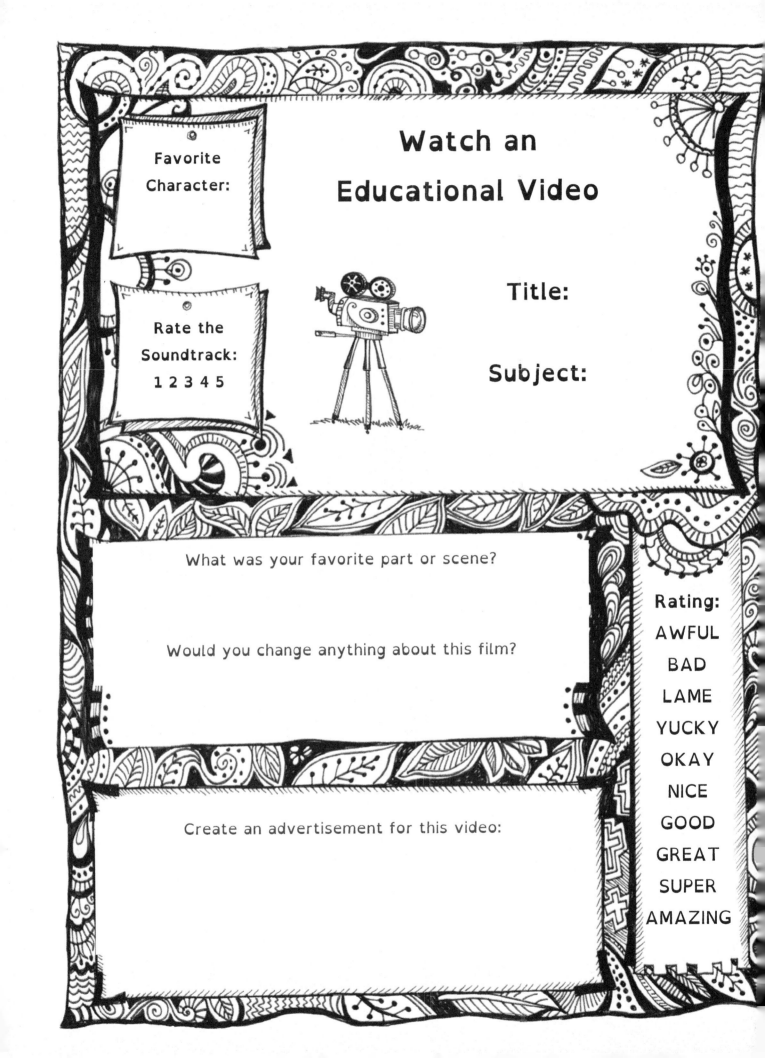

Use THIS PAGE for Math Practice
Or be creative and design something, like a house! You could make graphs, maps or geometric designs with this graph paper.

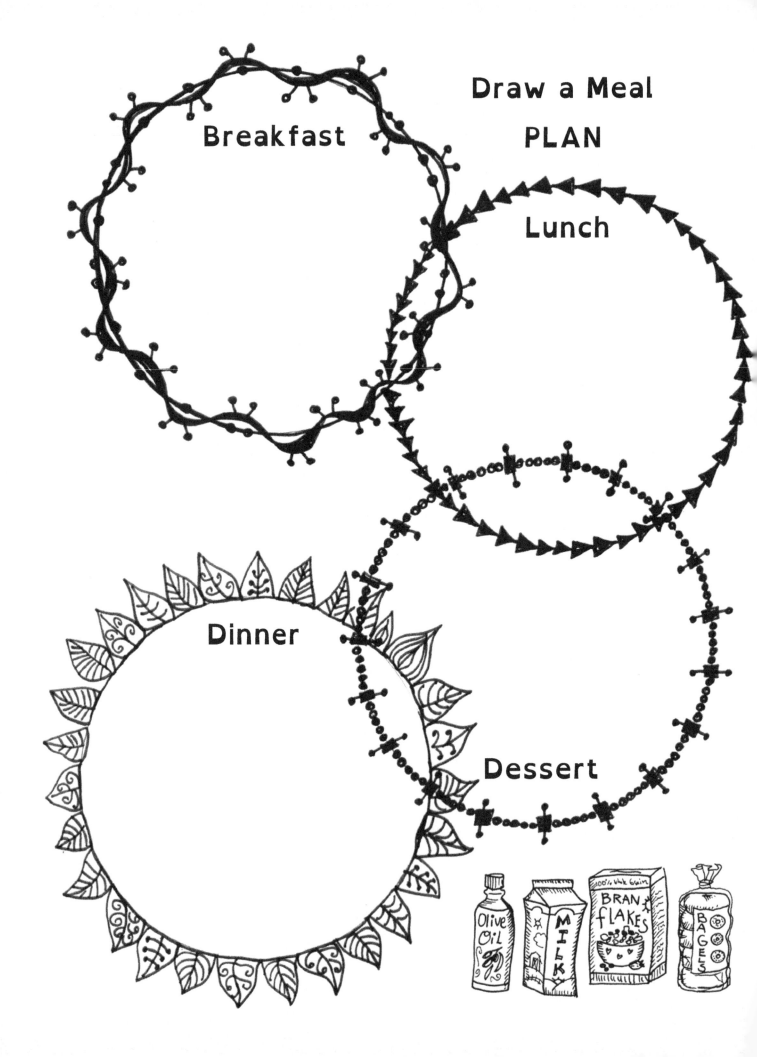

Book Time

Find an interesting sentence in one of your books and copy it. Draw a picture to go with the words.

TITLE: _____

Page Number: _____

Today's Date:_____

Copy a Verse or Quote

_____
_____
_____
_____
_____

My Plans:

_____
_____
_____
_____

To-Do List

_____
_____
_____
_____
_____
_____

LETTER DOODLES

Practice working with your colored pencils and learn to draw amazing letters too!

Object Lesson

Look at this picture.
List four things that you
can do with this object.

1. _____
2. _____
3. _____
4. _____

How are you feeling today?
Color the facial expressions that match your mood.

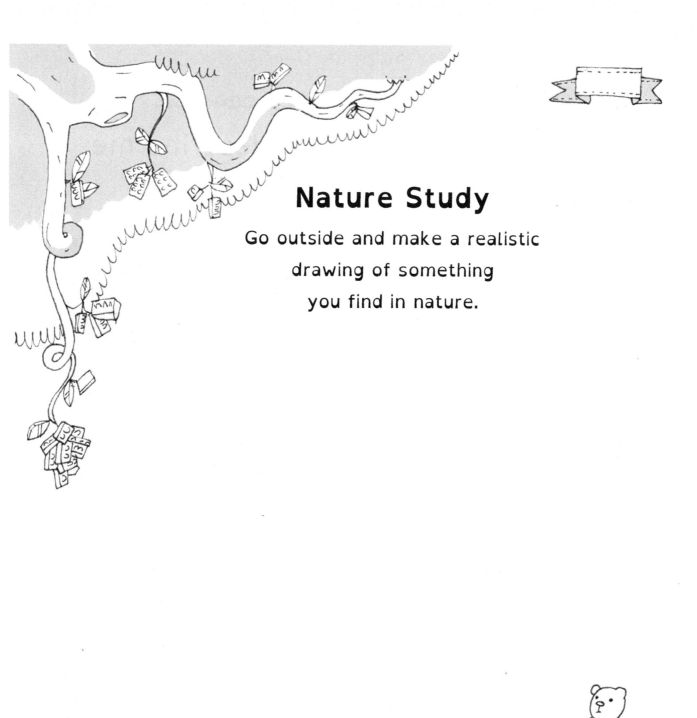

Nature Study

Go outside and make a realistic drawing of something you find in nature.

Color me with colored pencils.
Write just one word to describe me:

_____

Reading Time - 1 Hour (Set a timer)

Choose Four Books - Read from each book for 15 minutes.

Copy important words or pictures from each book here:

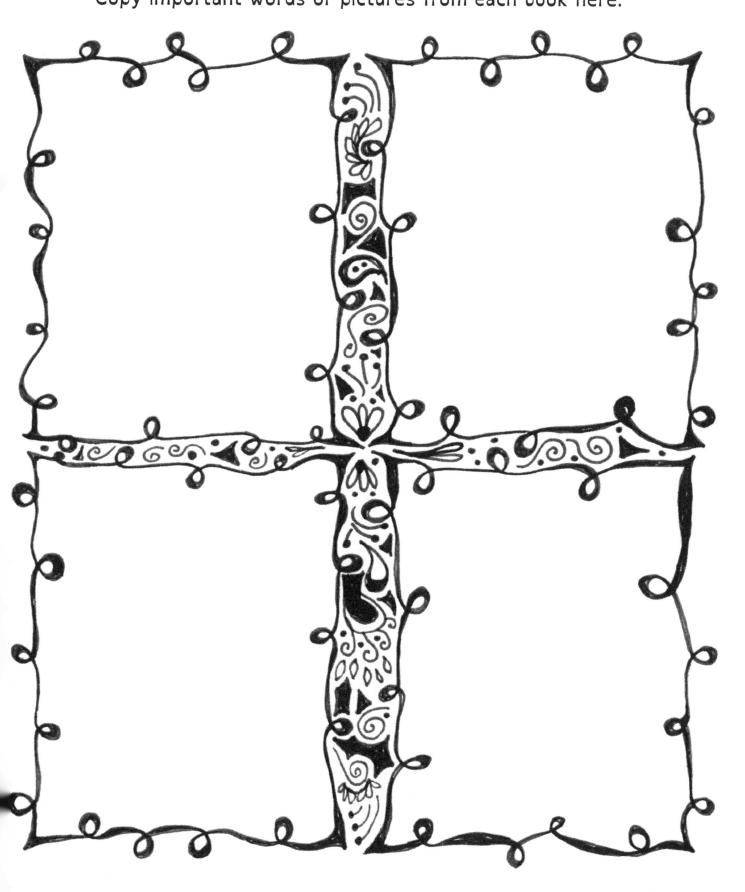

Write Today's Date: _____

Color the picture and write a story about it.

Spelling Time

Find 20 Words with **8** letters each.
Look in your books for words.
Write the words here:

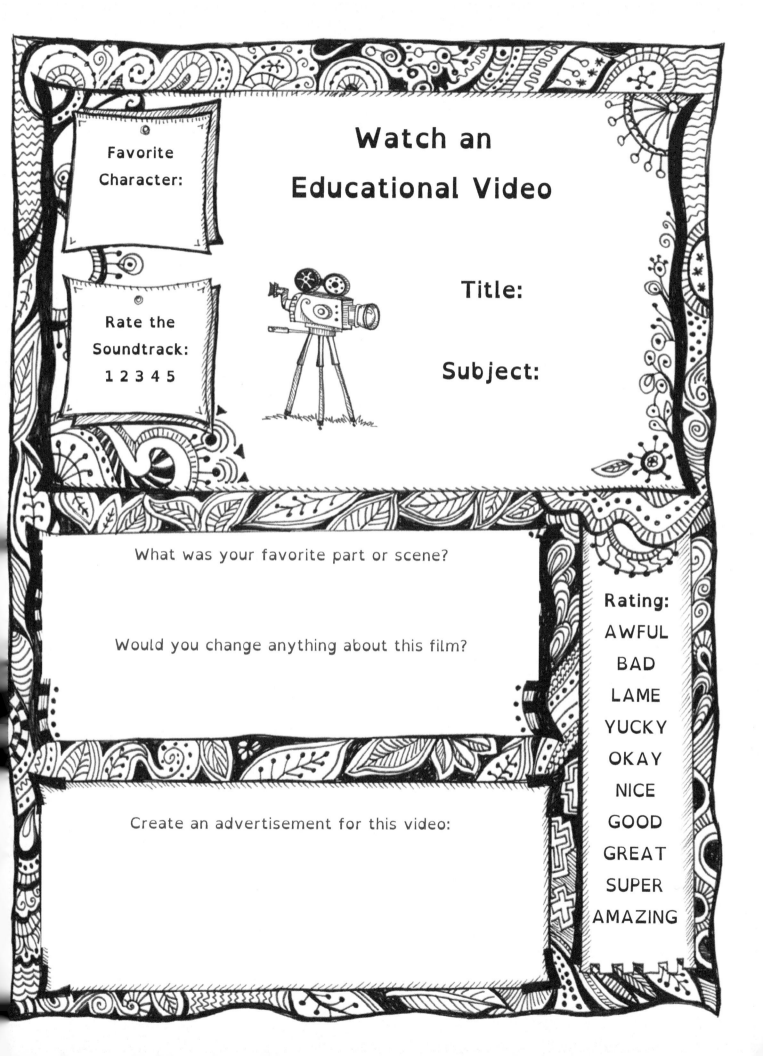

Use THIS PAGE for Math Practice

Or be creative and design something, like a house! You could make graphs, maps or geometric designs with this graph paper.

Animal Quiz

How much do you know about this animal?

Can you draw the animal's habitat, food and enemies?

Book Time

Find an interesting sentence in one of your books and copy it. Draw a picture to go with the words.

TITLE: _____

Page Number: _____

Thinking Time!
Can you complete the puzzle?

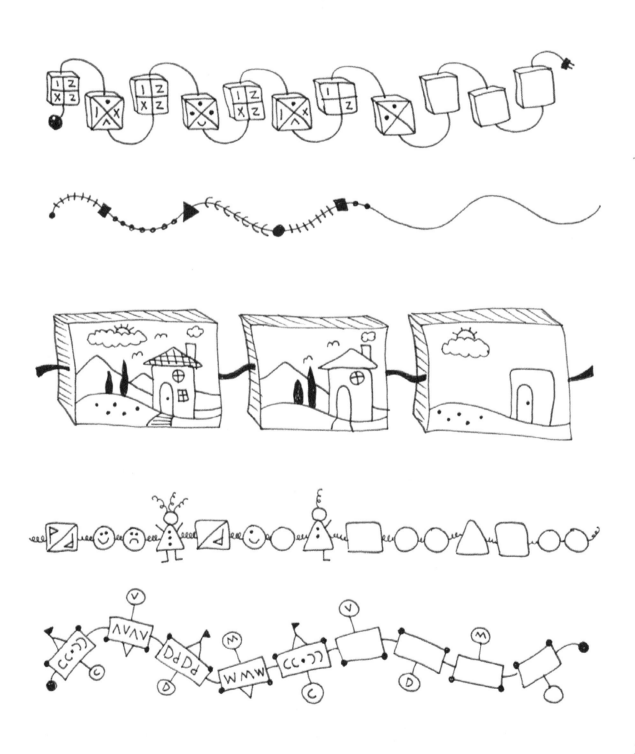

Today's Date:_____

Copy a Verse or Quote
_____
_____
_____
_____
_____

My Plans:
_____
_____
_____
_____

To-Do List
_____
_____
_____
_____
_____
_____

LETTER DOODLES

Practice working with your colored pencils and learn to draw amazing letters too!

Object Lesson

Look at this picture.
List four things that you
can do with this object.

1. _____
2. _____
3. _____
4. _____

Reading Time - 1 Hour (Set a timer)

Choose Four Books - Read from each book for 15 minutes.

Copy important words or pictures from each book here:

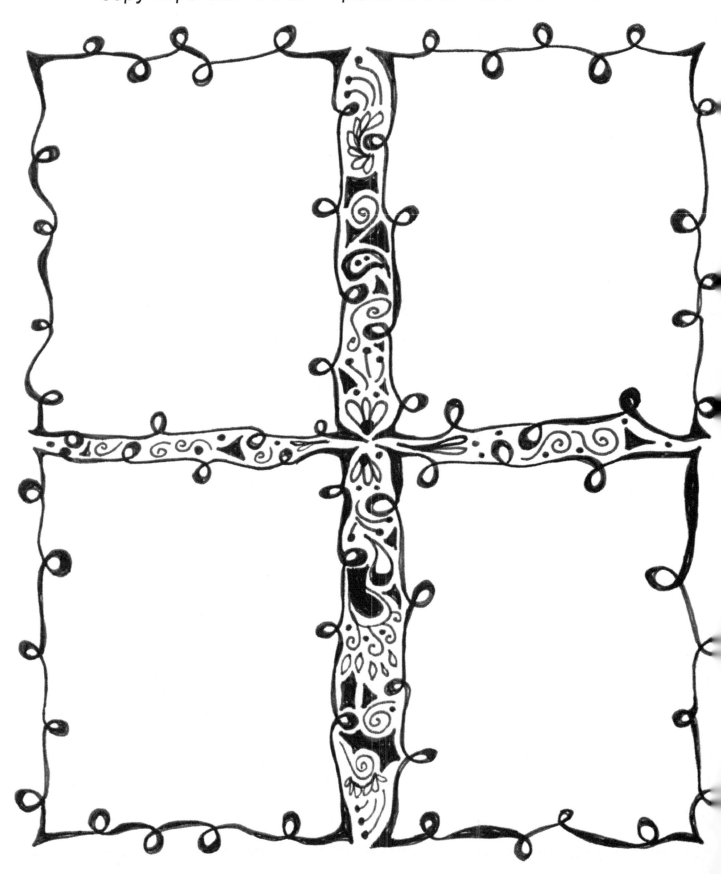

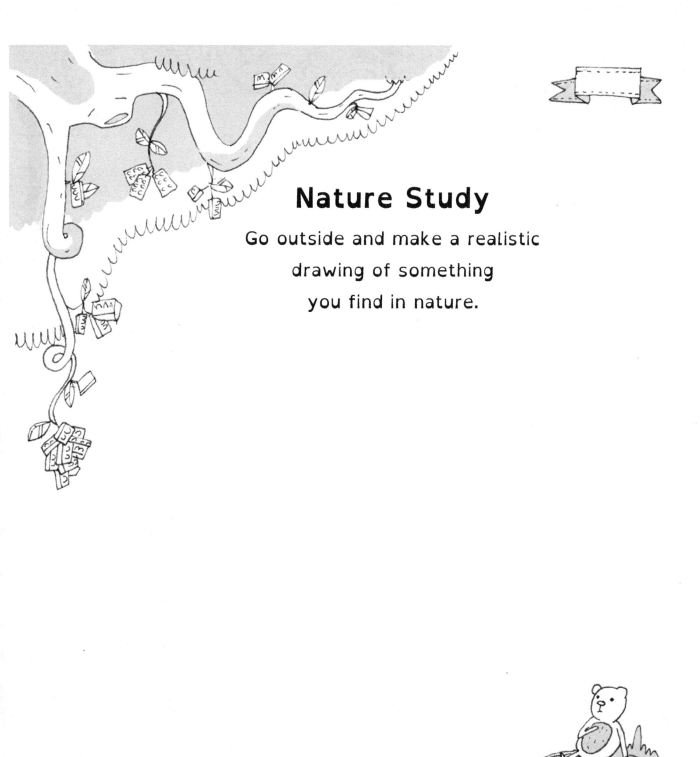

Nature Study

Go outside and make a realistic drawing of something you find in nature.

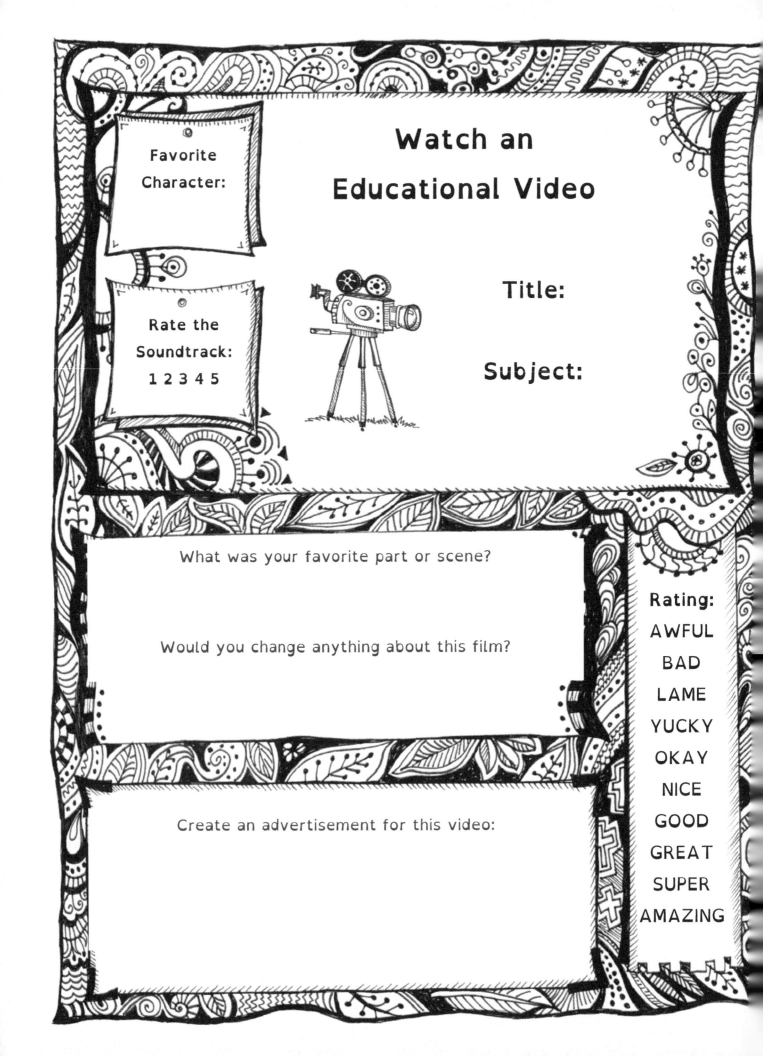

Use THIS PAGE for Math Practice
Or be creative and design something, like a house! You could make graphs, maps or geometric designs with this graph paper.

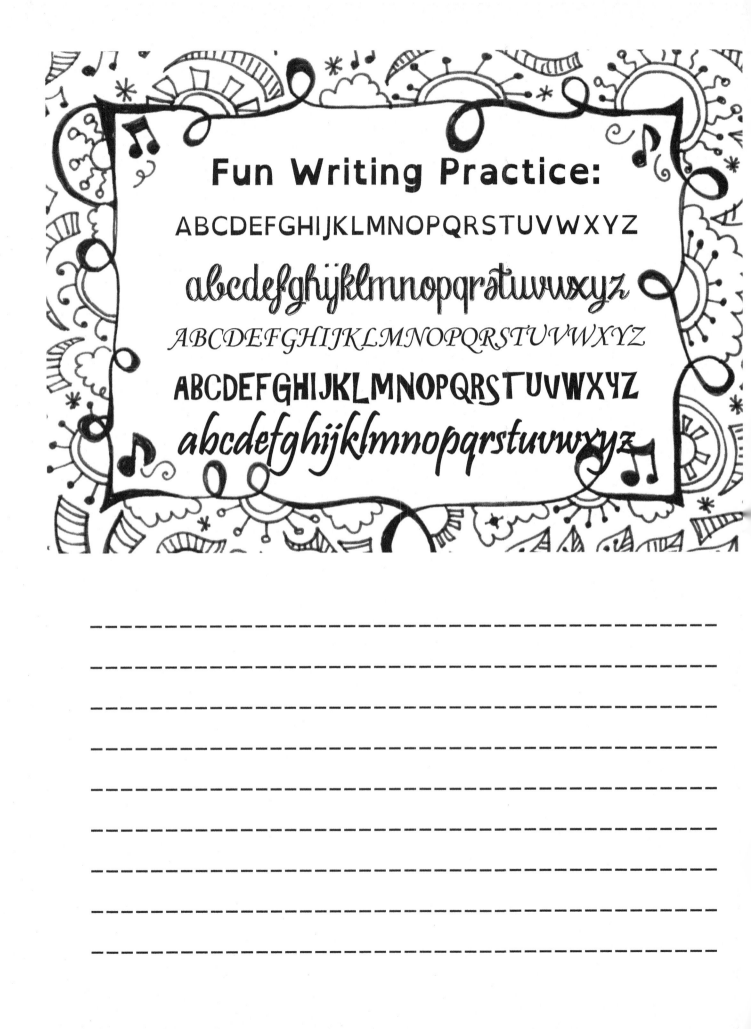

Book Time

Find an interesting sentence in one of your books and copy it. Draw a picture to go with the words.

TITLE:_____

Page Number:_____

Reading Time - 1 Hour (Set a timer)

Choose Four Books - Read from each book for 15 minutes.

Copy important words or pictures from each book here:

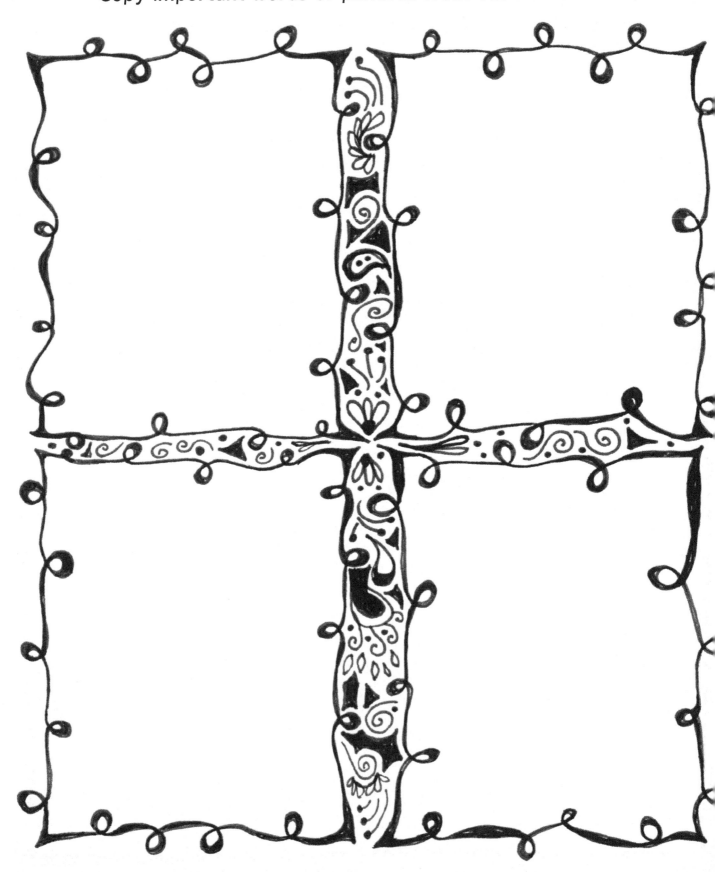

Spelling Time

Find 20 Words with 7 letters each.
Look in your books for words.
Write the words here:

LETTER DOODLES

Practice working with your colored pencils and learn to draw amazing letters too!

Object Lesson

Look at this picture.
List four things that you
can do with this object.

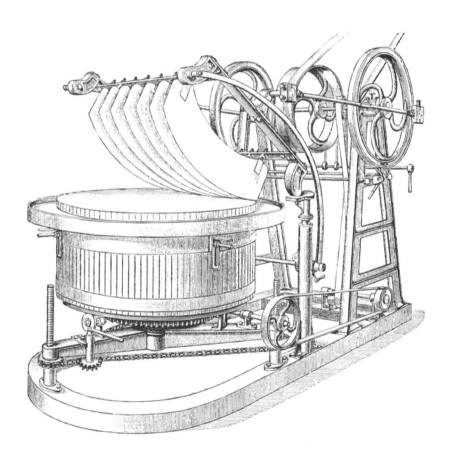

1._____
2._____
3._____
4._____

Today's Date:_____

Copy a Verse or Quote

My Plans:

To-Do List

Write Today's Date: _____

Color the picture and write a story about it.

How are you feeling today?
Circle all the facial expressions that best depict your moods today.

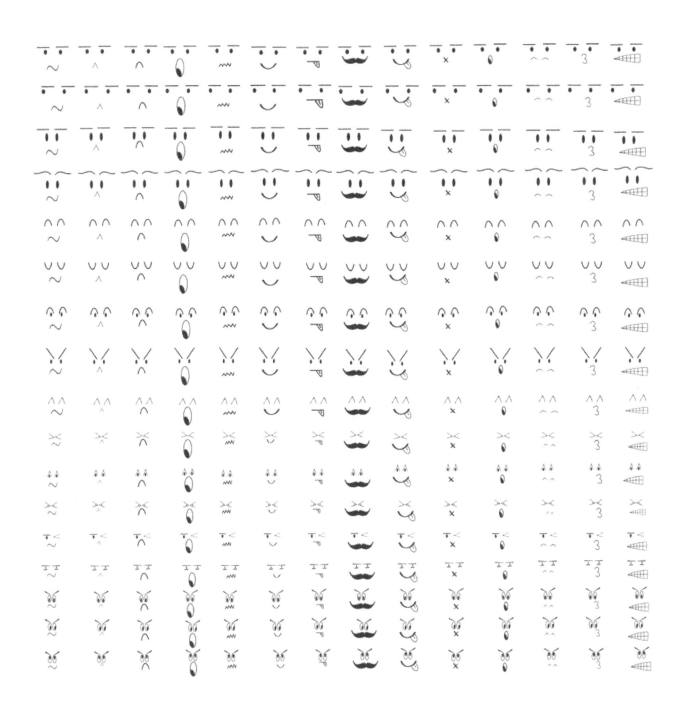

Color me with colored pencils.

Write just one word to describe me:

_____

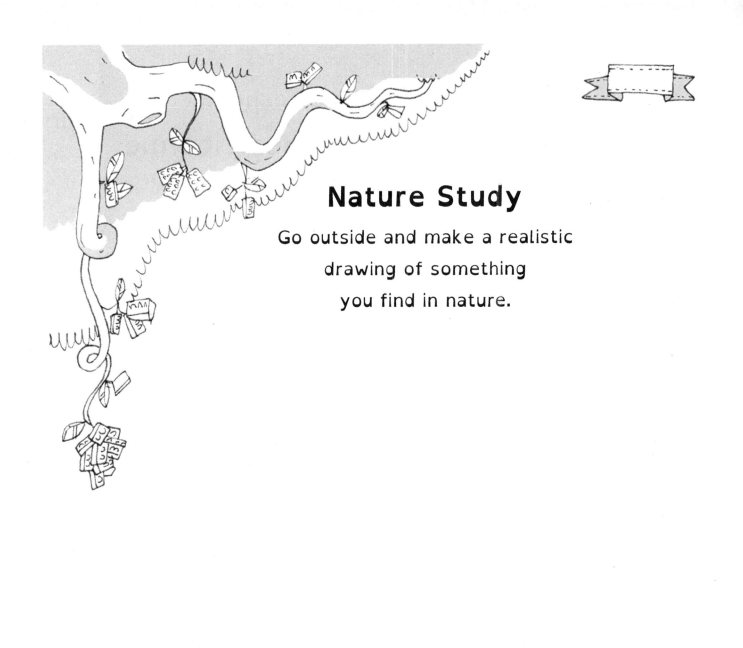

Nature Study

Go outside and make a realistic drawing of something you find in nature.

Reading Time - 1 Hour (Set a timer)

Choose Four Books - Read from each book for 15 minutes.

Copy important words or pictures from each book here:

Spelling Time

Find 20 Words with 6 letters each.
Look in your books for words.
Write the words here:

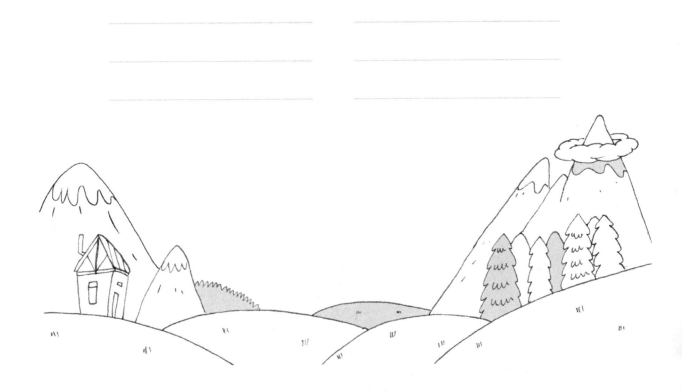

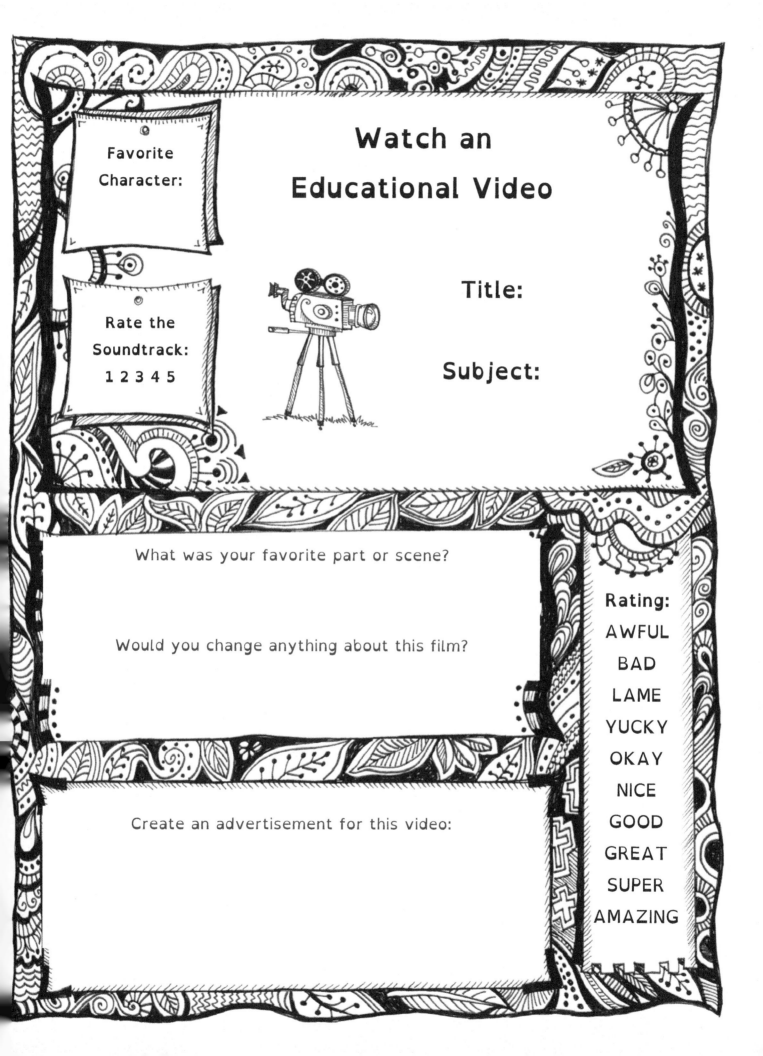

Use THIS PAGE for Math Practice

Or be creative and design something, like a house! You could make graphs, maps or geometric designs with this graph paper.

Book Time

Find an interesting sentence in one of your books and copy it. Draw a picture to go with the words.

TITLE:_____

Page Number:_____

Thinking Time!

Can you complete the puzzle?

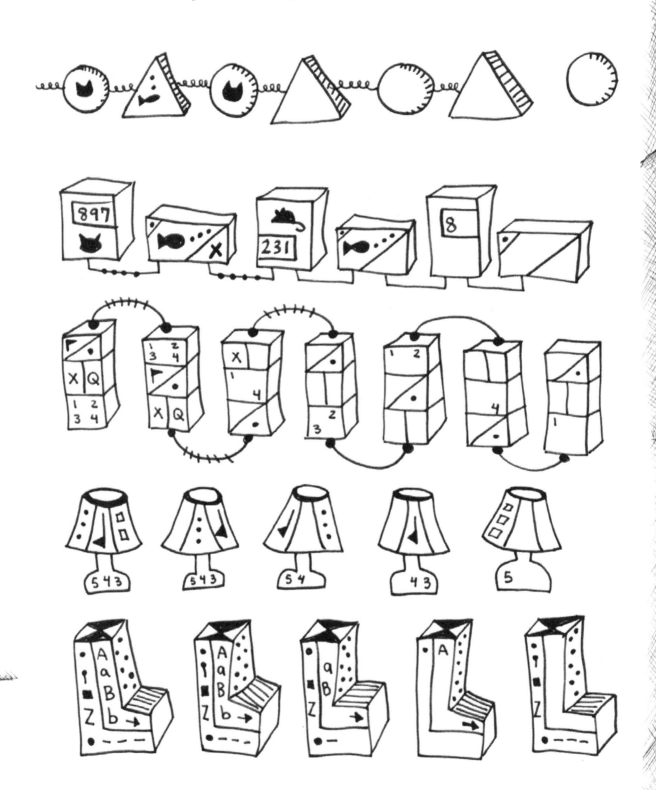

Today's Date:_____

Copy a Verse or Quote

_____
_____
_____
_____
_____

My Plans:

_____
_____
_____
_____

To-Do List

_____
_____
_____
_____
_____
_____

LETTER DOODLES

Practice working with your colored pencils and learn to draw amazing letters too!

Object Lesson

Look at this picture.
List four things that you
can do with this object.

1. _____
2. _____
3. _____
4. _____

How are you feeling today?
Color the facial expressions that match your mood.

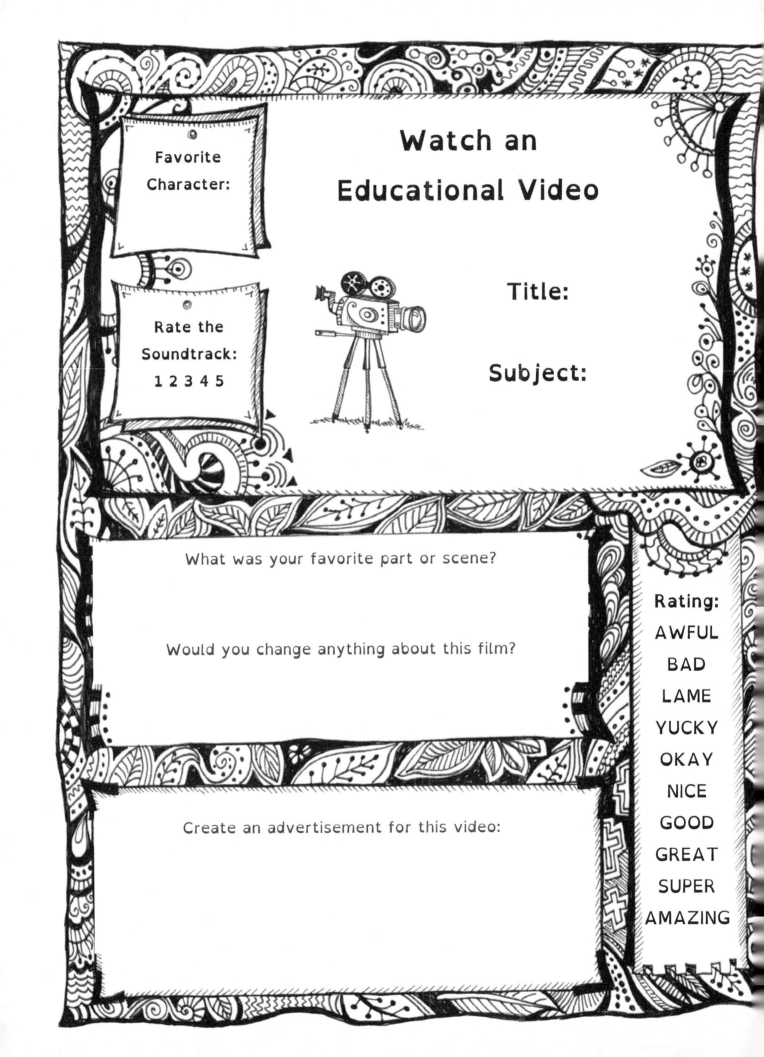

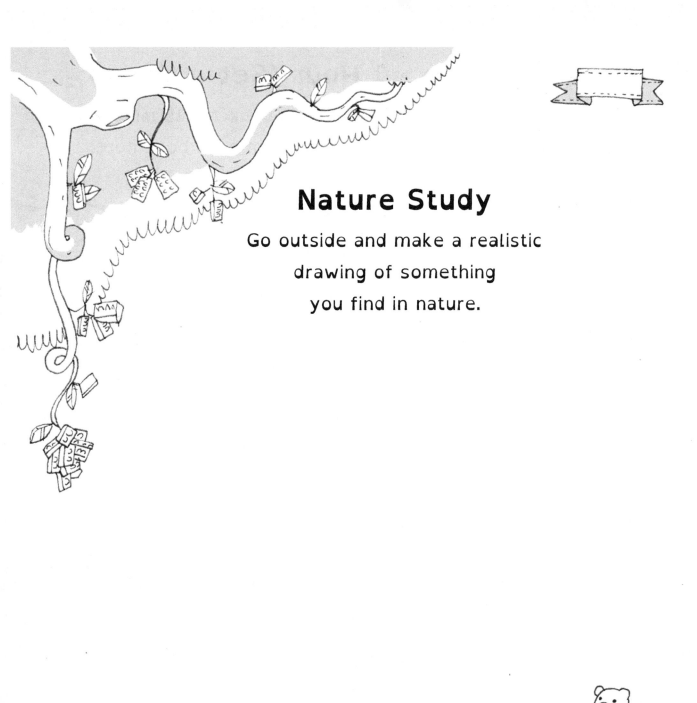

Nature Study

Go outside and make a realistic drawing of something you find in nature.

Reading Time - 1 Hour (Set a timer)

Choose Four Books - Read from each book for 15 minutes.

Copy important words or pictures from each book here:

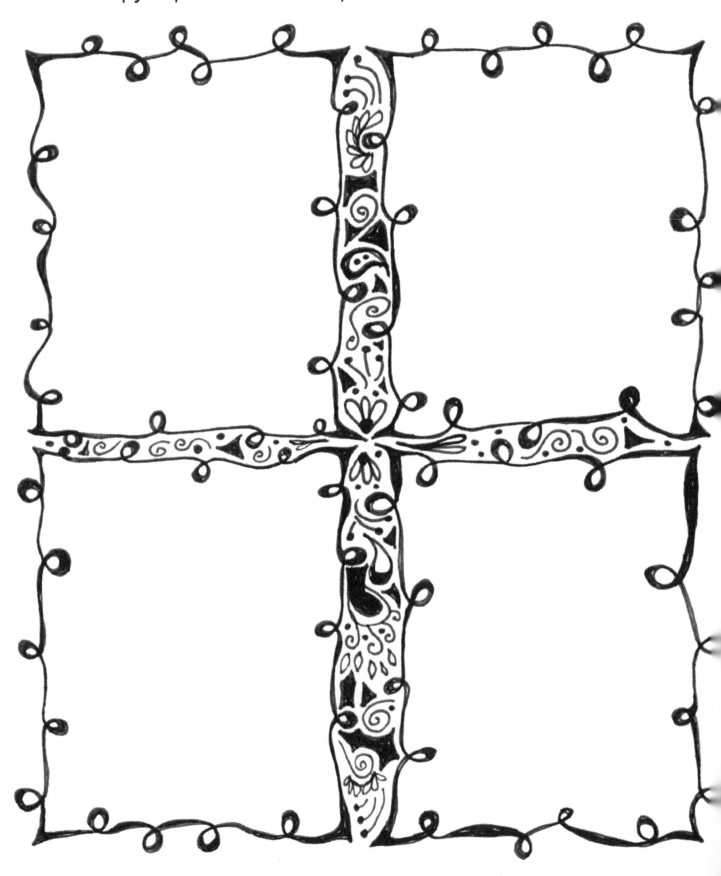

Spelling Time

Find 20 Words with 5 letters each.
Look in your books for words.
Write the words here:

World News Today!

Talk to your parents about current events.
Look at a newspaper, news broadcast or website.
Tell the news stories with words and pictures.

WHO:

WHAT:

WHEN:

WHERE:

WHY:

Book Time

Find an interesting sentence in one of your books and copy it. Draw a picture to go with the words.

TITLE:_____

Page Number:_____

Color the picture and write a story about it.

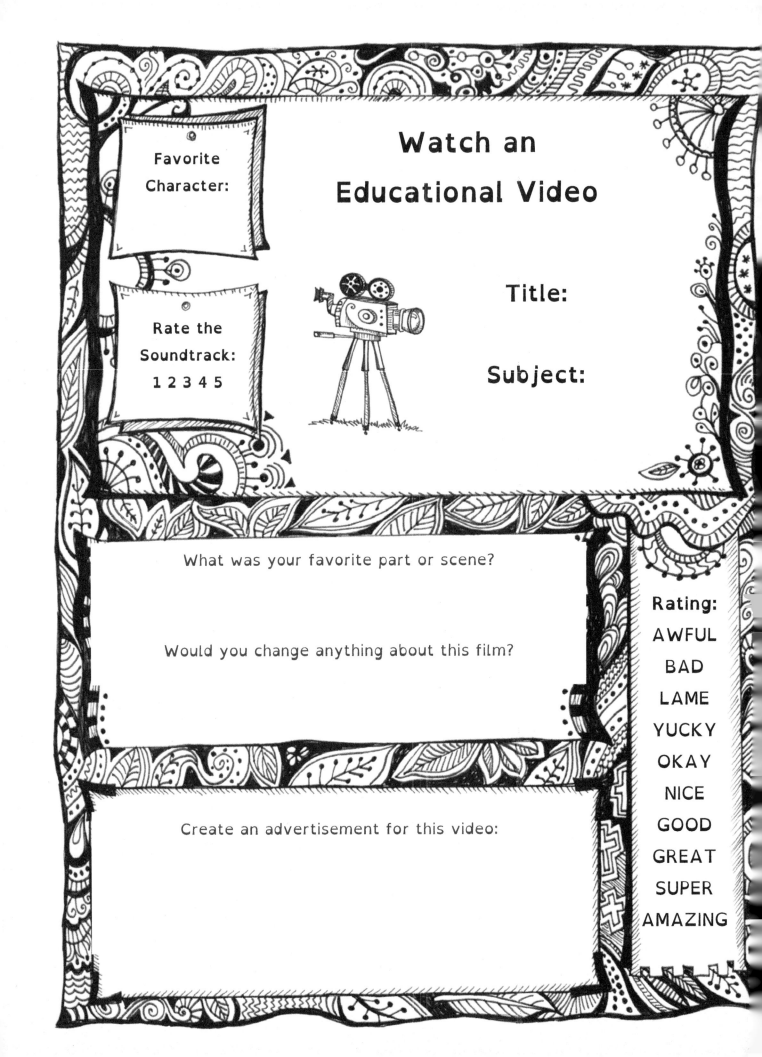

Use THIS PAGE for Math Practice

Or be creative and design something, like a house! You could make graphs, maps or geometric designs with this graph paper.

Thinking Time!

Can you complete the puzzle?

Color me with colored pencils.
Write just one word to describe me:
_____

Today's Date:_____

Copy a Verse or Quote

My Plans:

To-Do List

LETTER DOODLES

Practice working with your colored pencils and learn to draw amazing letters too!

Object Lesson

Look at this picture.
List four things that you
can do with this object.

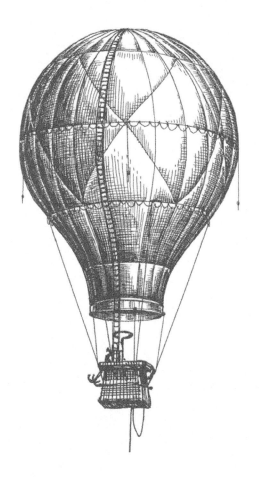

1. _____
2. _____
3. _____
4. _____

How are you feeling today?
Color the facial expression

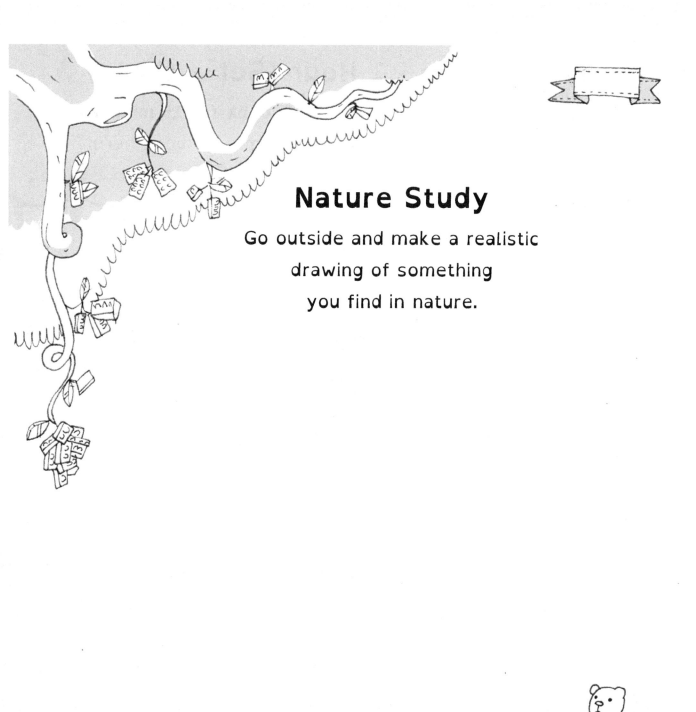

Nature Study

Go outside and make a realistic drawing of something you find in nature.

Reading Time - 1 Hour (Set a timer)

Choose Four Books - Read from each book for 15 minutes.

Copy important words or pictures from each book here:

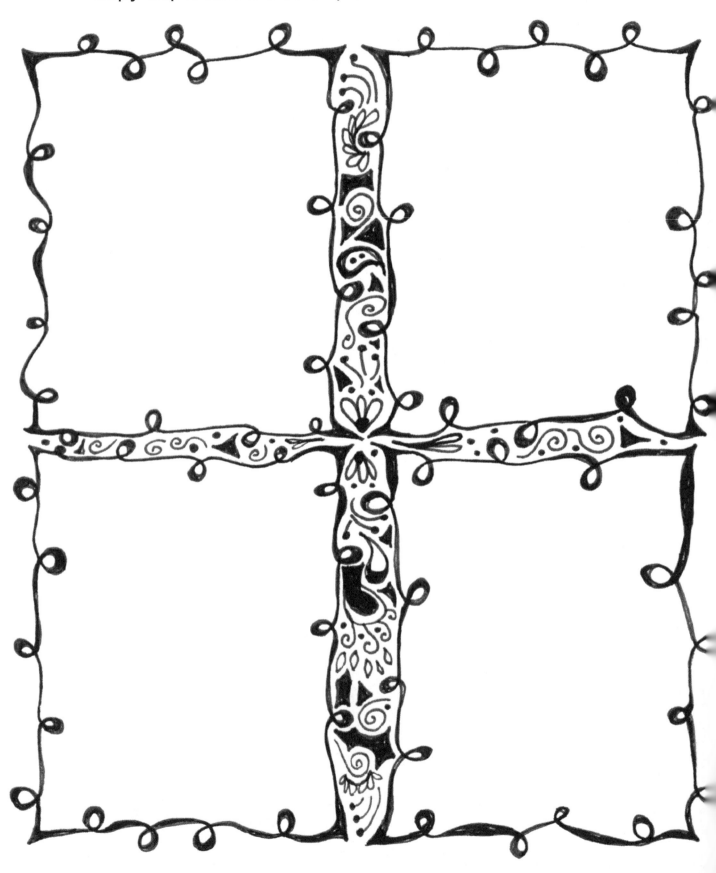

Spelling Time

Find 20 Words with **6** letters each.
Look in your books for words.
Write the words here:

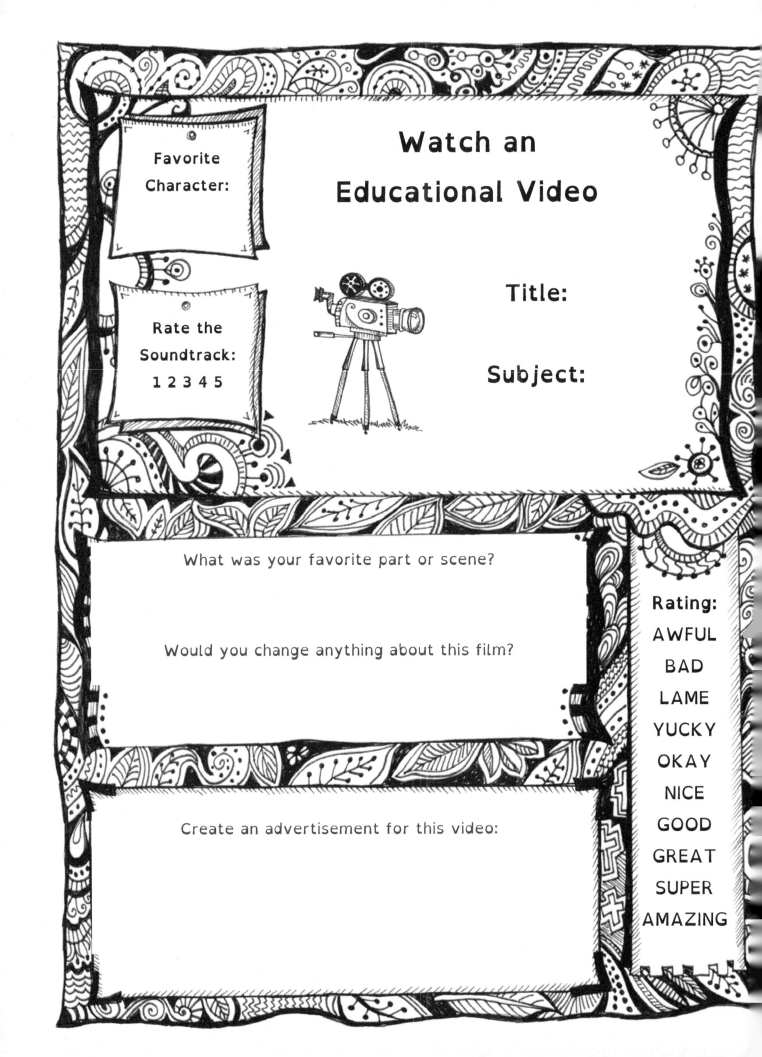

Use THIS PAGE for Math Practice
Or be creative and design something, like a house! You could make graphs, maps or geometric designs with this graph paper.

Listening Time

Listen to an audio book or classical music or ask someone to read a story to you while you color and draw on the next page.

What are you listening to?

_____

Color me with colored pencils.

Write just one word to describe me:

Thinking Time!

Can you complete the puzzle?

Today's Date:_____

Copy a Verse or Quote

_____
_____
_____
_____
_____

My Plans:

_____
_____
_____
_____

To-Do List

_____
_____
_____
_____
_____
_____

Object Lesson

Look at this picture.
List four things that you
can do with this object.

1. _____
2. _____
3. _____
4. _____

How are you feeling today?

Color the facial expressions that match your mood.

Color the picture and write a story about it.

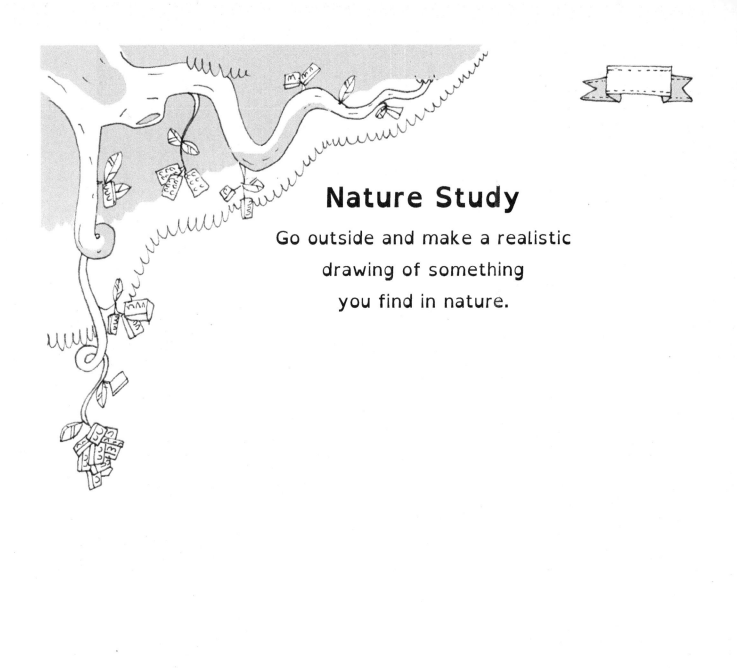

Nature Study

Go outside and make a realistic drawing of something you find in nature.

Reading Time - 1 Hour (Set a timer)

Choose Four Books - Read from each book for 15 minutes.

Copy important words or pictures from each book here:

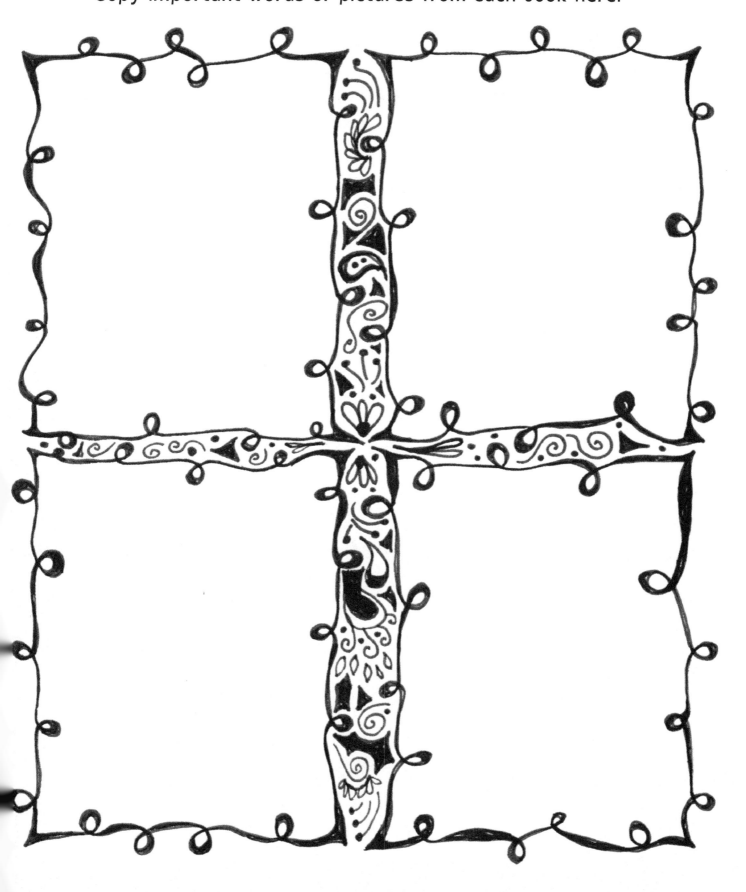

Spelling Time

Find 20 Words with 7 letters each.
Look in your books for words.
Write the words here:

Color me with colored pencils.
Write just one word to describe me:

_____

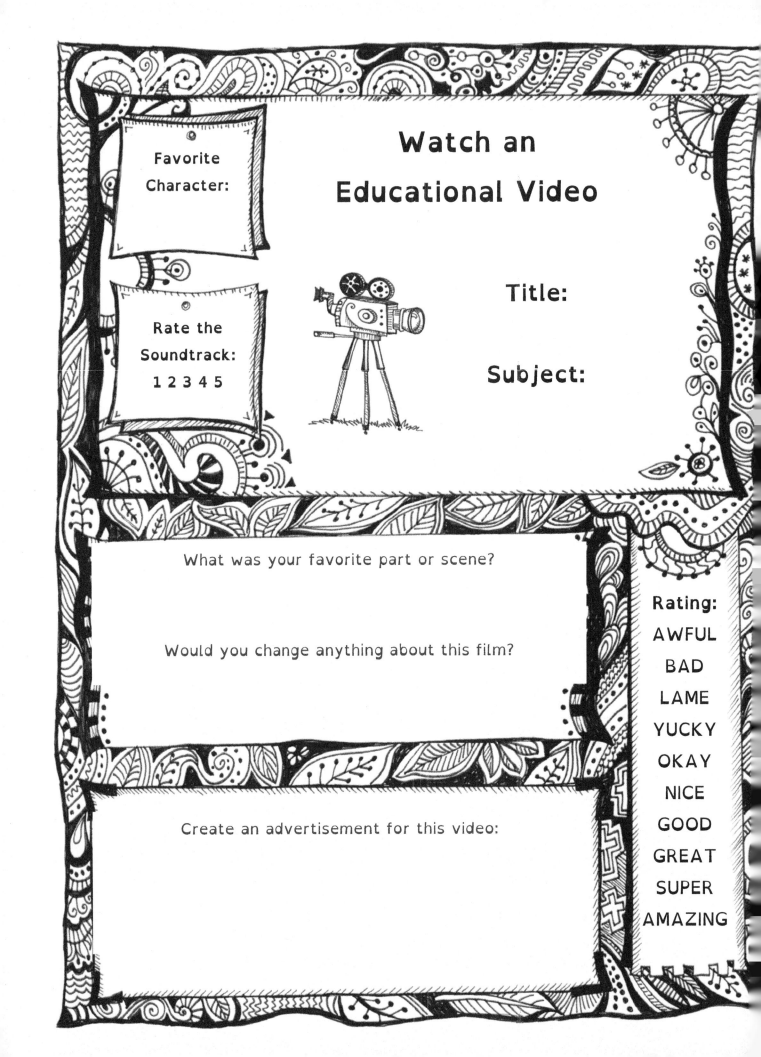

Use THIS PAGE for Math Practice
Or be creative and design something, like a house! You could make graphs, maps or geometric designs with this graph paper.

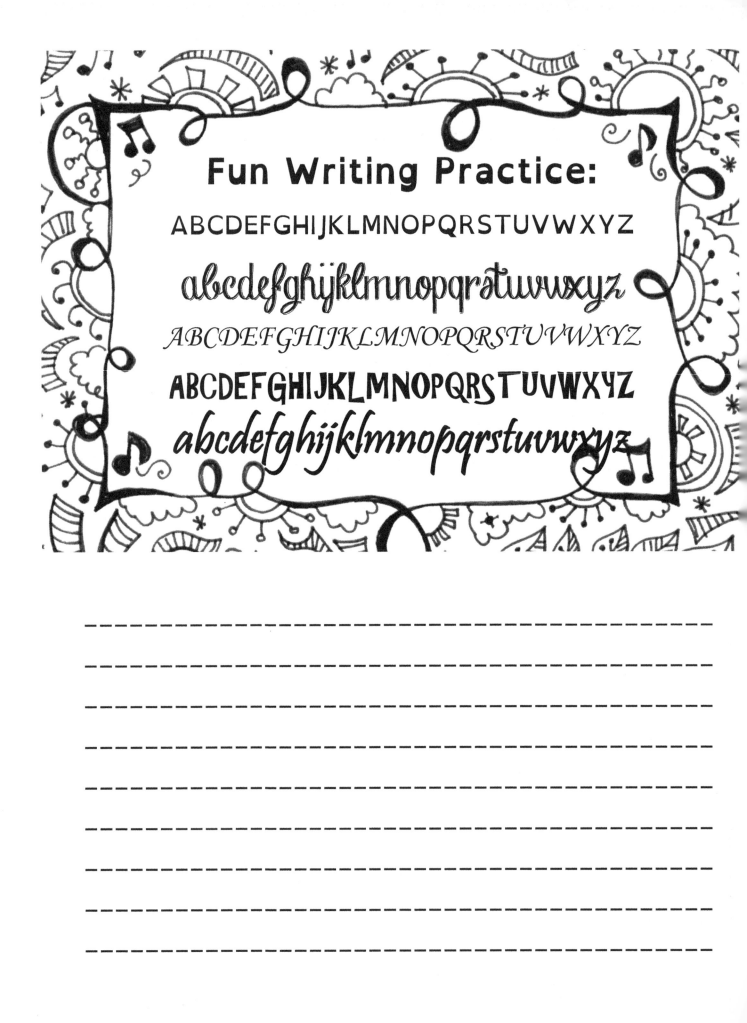

Book Time

Find an interesting sentence in one of your books and copy it. Draw a picture to go with the words.

TITLE:_____

Page Number:_____

Today's Date:_____

Copy a Verse or Quote

My Plans:

To-Do List

Thinking Time!

Can you complete the puzzle?

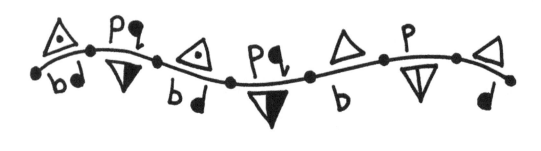

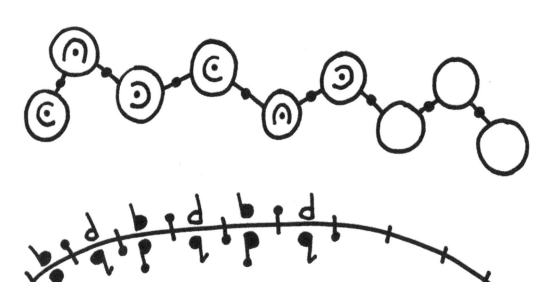

Object Lesson

Look at this picture.
List four things that you
can do with this object.

1. _____
2. _____
3. _____
4. _____

How are you feeling today?

Circle all the facial expressions
that best depict your moods today.

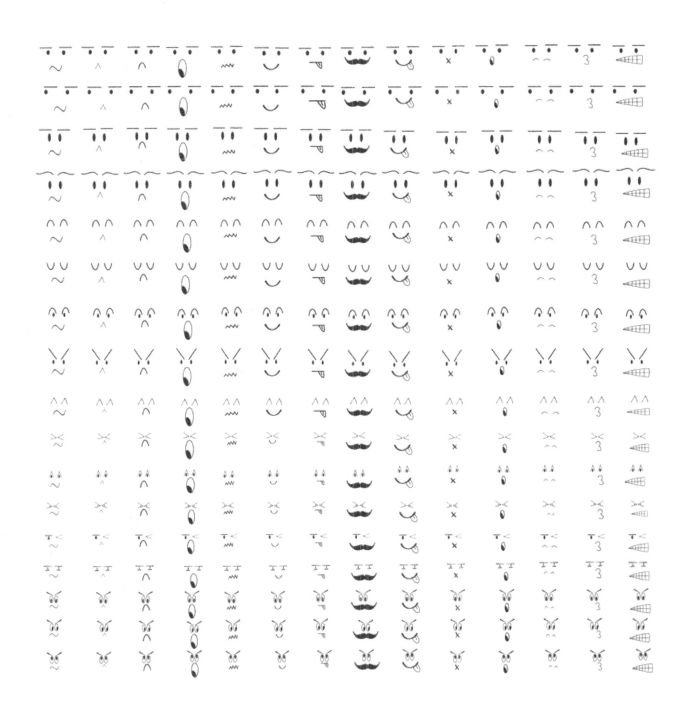

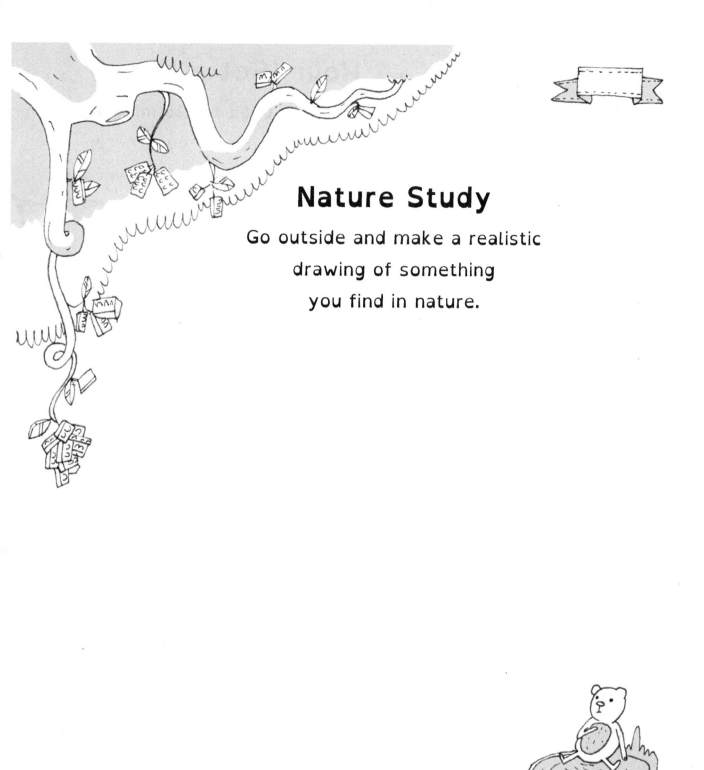

Nature Study

Go outside and make a realistic drawing of something you find in nature.

Reading Time - 1 Hour (Set a timer)

Choose Four Books - Read from each book for 15 minutes.

Copy important words or pictures from each book here:

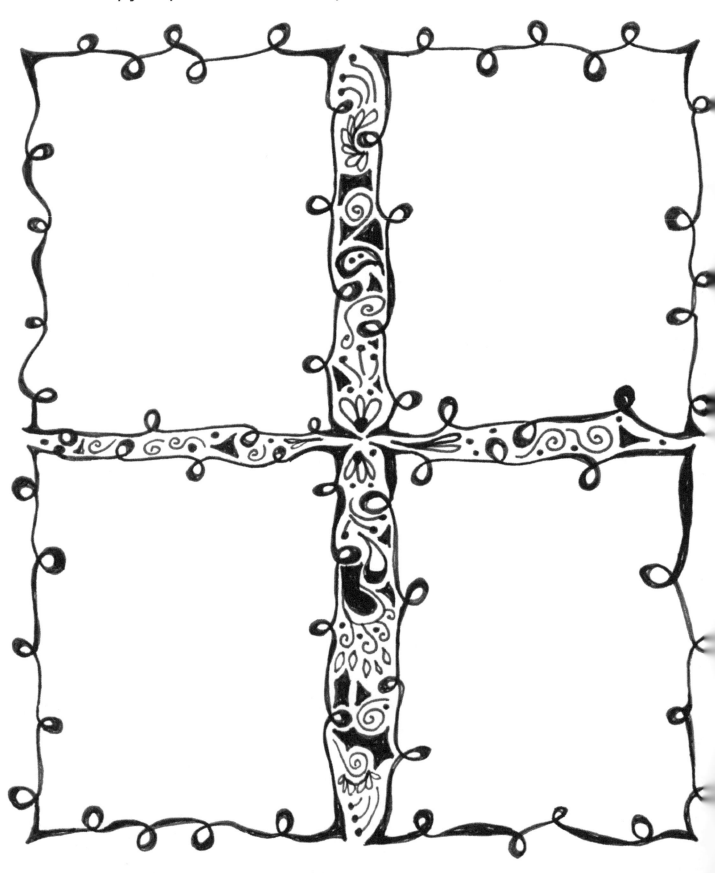

Color me with colored pencils.
Write just one word to describe me:

_____

Spelling Time

Find 20 Words with **8** letters each.
Look in your books for words.
Write the words here:

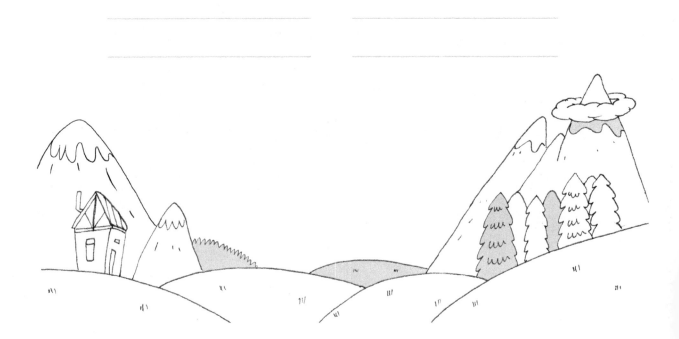

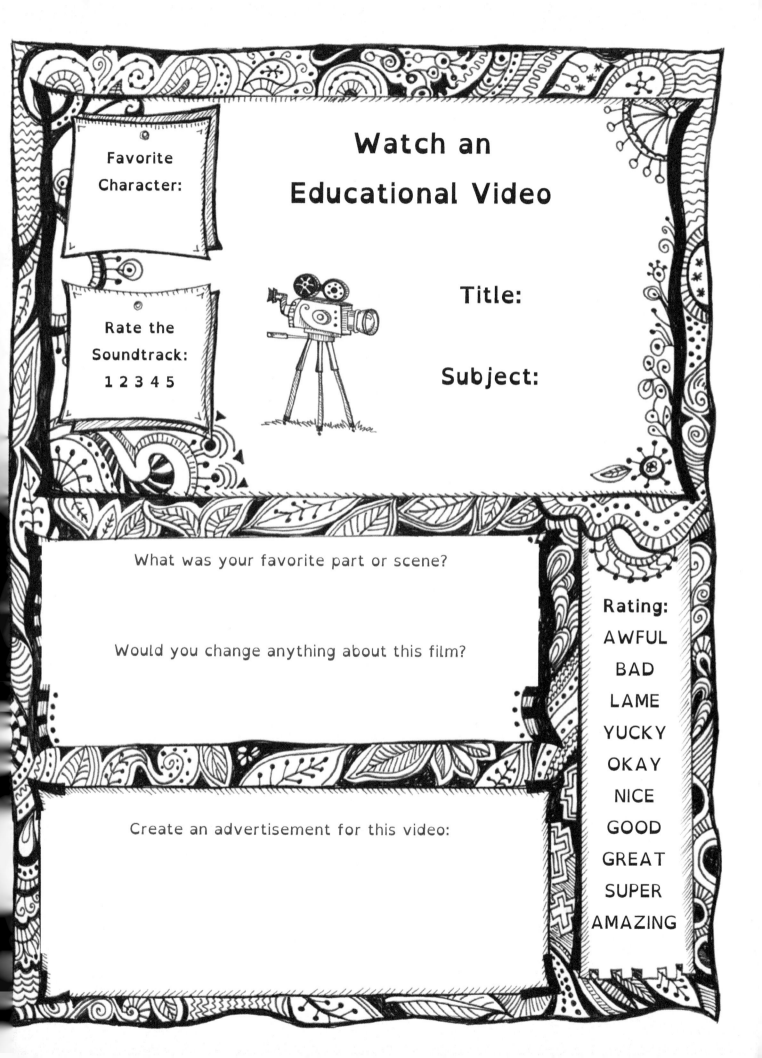

Color the picture and write a story about it.

Use THIS PAGE for Math Practice
Or be creative and design something, like a house! You could make graphs, maps or geometric designs with this graph paper.

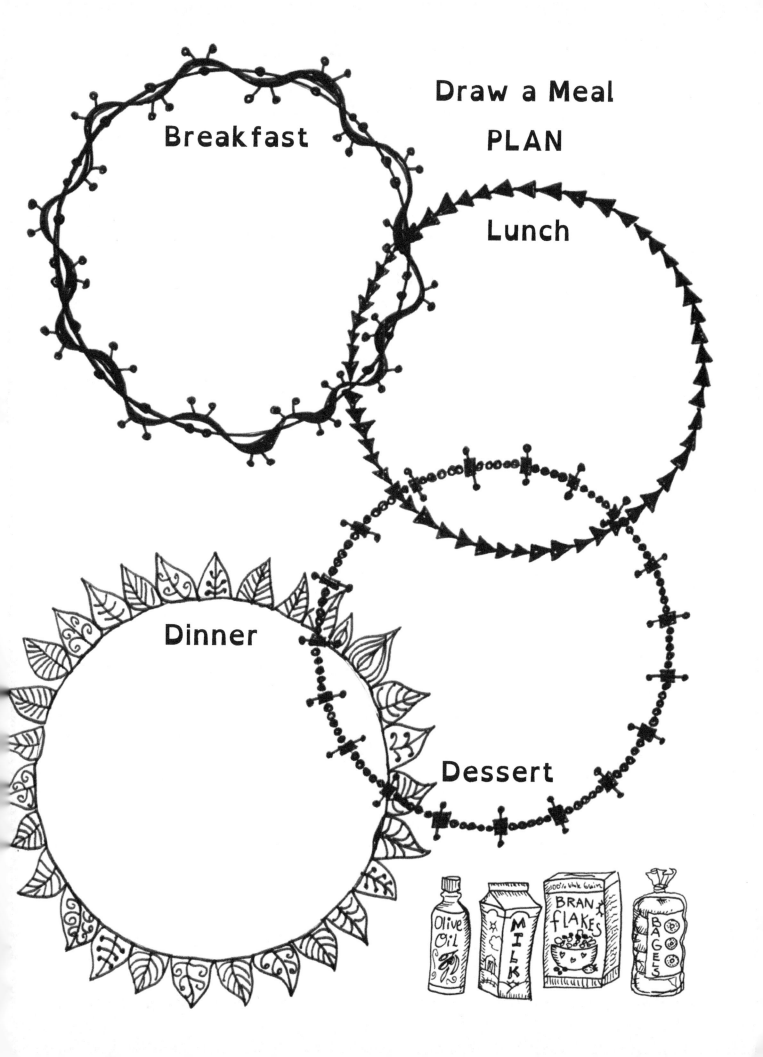

Book Time

Find an interesting sentence in one of your books and copy it. Draw a picture to go with the words.

TITLE:_____

Page Number:_____

Thinking Time!
Can you complete the puzzle?

Today's Date:_____

Copy a Verse or Quote

My Plans:

To-Do List

Object Lesson

Look at this picture.
List four things that you
can do with this object.

1. _____
2. _____
3. _____
4. _____

How are you feeling today?
Color the facial expression

Color me with colored pencils.
Write just one word to describe me:

_____

Nature Study

Go outside and make a realistic drawing of something you find in nature.

Reading Time - 1 Hour (Set a timer)

Choose Four Books - Read from each book for 15 minutes.

Copy important words or pictures from each book here:

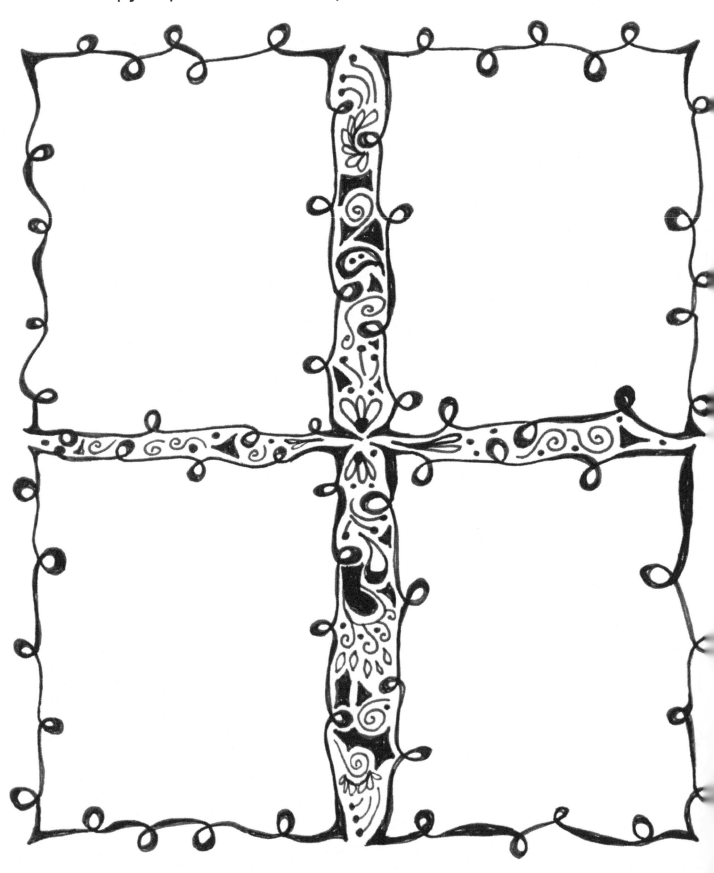

Spelling Time

Find 20 Words with 7 letters each.
Look in your books for words.
Write the words here:

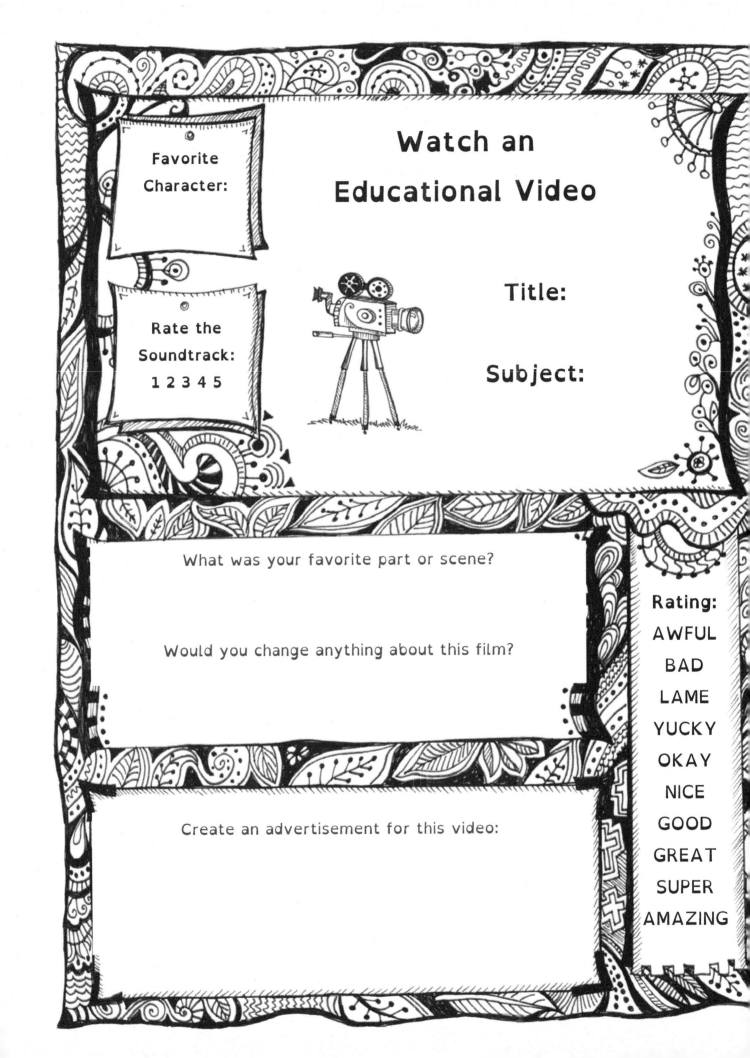

Use THIS PAGE for Math Practice
Or be creative and design something, like a house! You could make graphs, maps or geometric designs with this graph paper.

Animal Quiz

How much do you know about this animal?

Can you draw the animal's habitat, food and enemies?

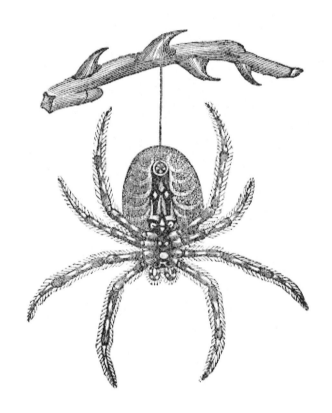

Book Time

Find an interesting sentence in one of your books and copy it. Draw a picture to go with the words.

TITLE:_____

Page Number:_____

Thinking Time!

Can you complete the puzzle?

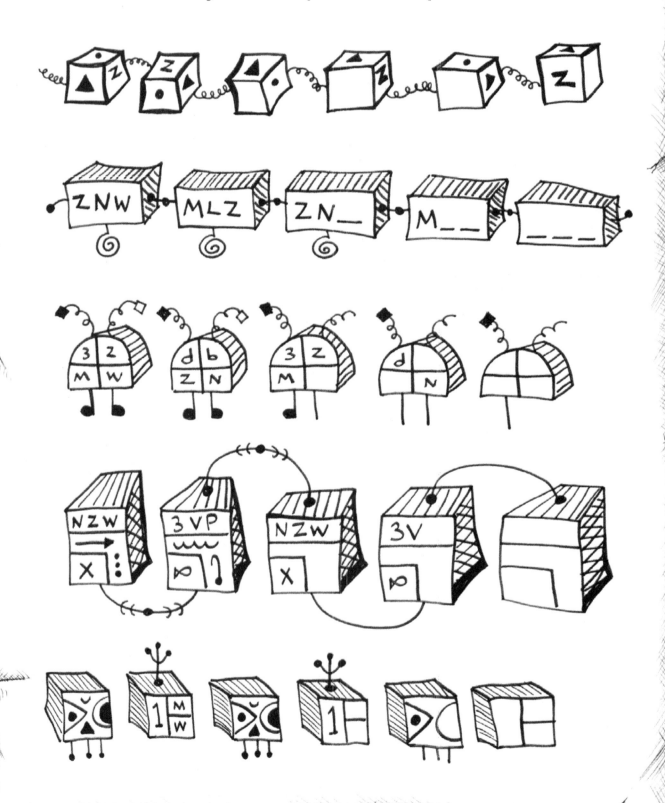

Color me with colored pencils.

Write just one word to describe me:

_____

Today's Date:_____

Copy a Verse or Quote
_____
_____
_____
_____
_____

My Plans:
_____
_____
_____
_____

To-Do List
_____
_____
_____
_____
_____
_____
_____

Color the picture and write a story about it.

Object Lesson

Look at this picture.
List four things that you
can do with this object.

1. _____
2. _____
3. _____
4. _____

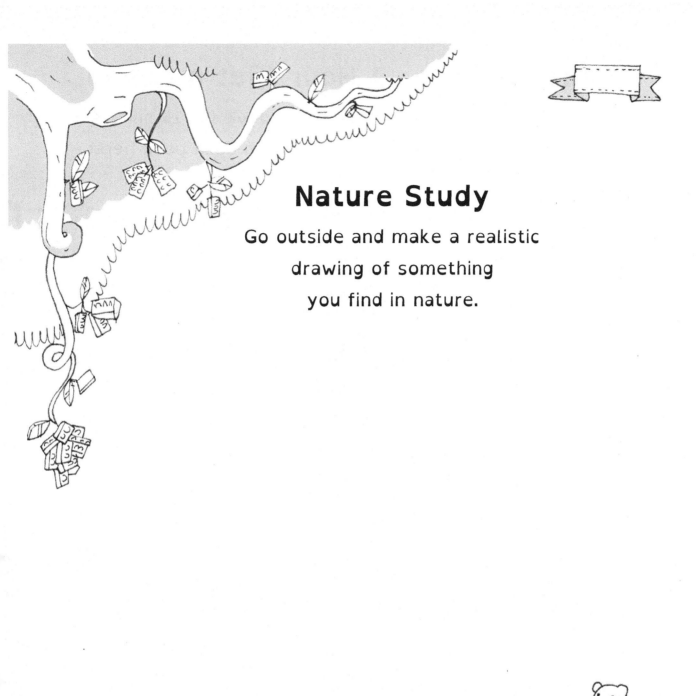

Nature Study

Go outside and make a realistic drawing of something you find in nature.

Reading Time - 1 Hour (Set a timer)

Choose Four Books - Read from each book for 15 minutes.

Copy important words or pictures from each book here:

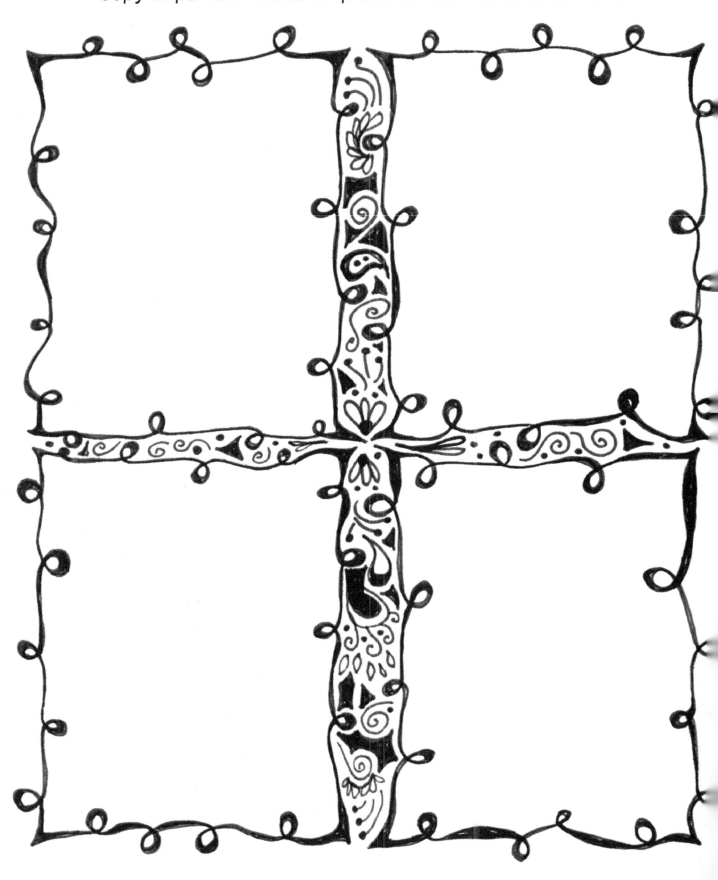

Spelling Time

Find 20 Words with 7 letters each.
Look in your books for words.
Write the words here:

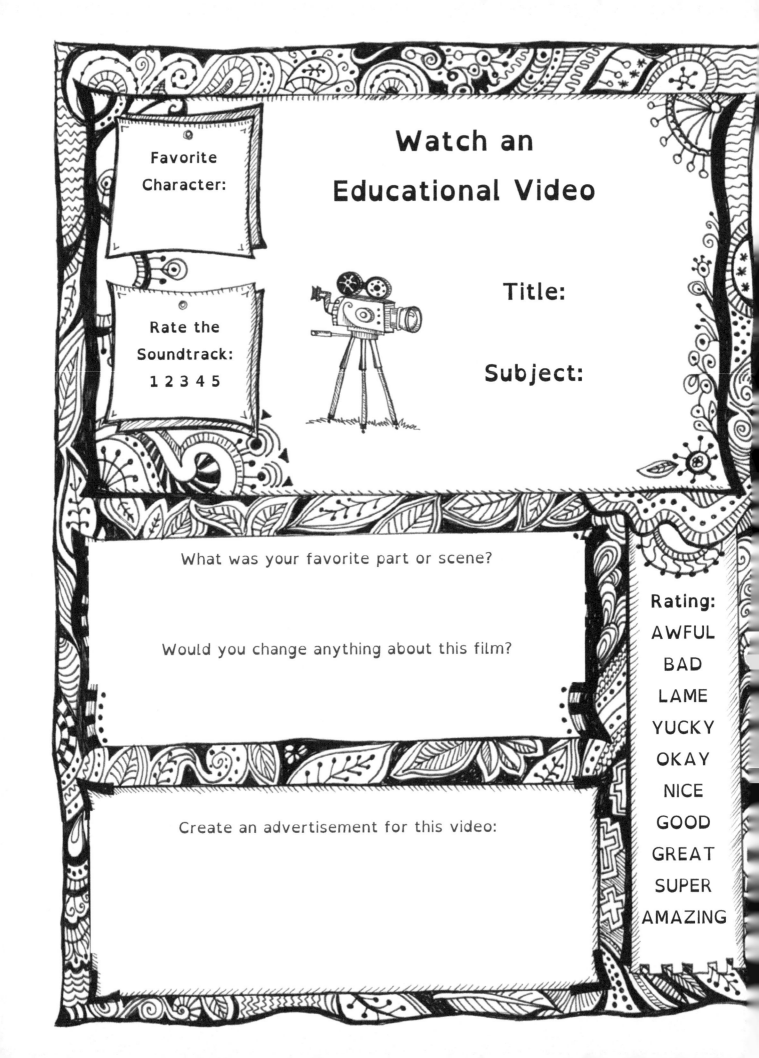

Use THIS PAGE for Math Practice
Or be creative and design something, like a house! You could make graphs, maps or geometric designs with this graph paper.

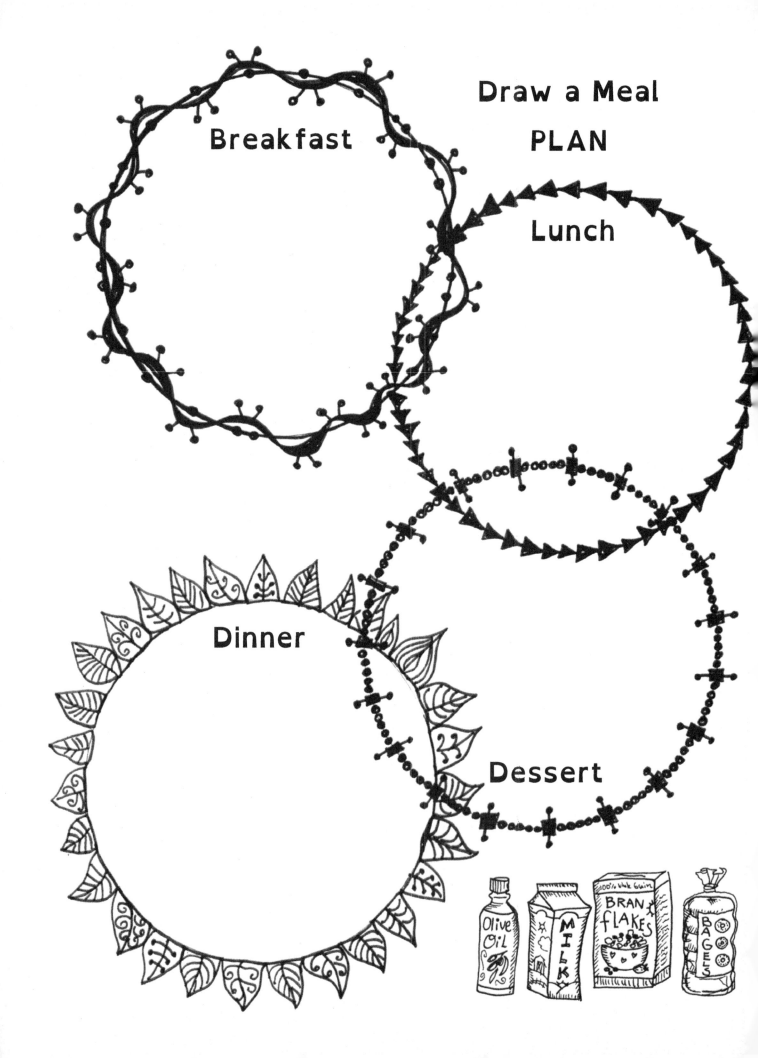

Book Time

Find an interesting sentence in one of your books and copy it. Draw a picture to go with the words.

TITLE:_____

Page Number:_____

Today's Date:_____

Copy a Verse or Quote

_____
_____
_____
_____
_____

My Plans:
_____
_____
_____
_____

To-Do List
_____
_____
_____
_____
_____
_____
_____

Object Lesson

Look at this picture.
List four things that you
can do with this object.

1. _____
2. _____
3. _____
4. _____

Color me with colored pencils.
Write just one word to describe me:

_____

This is the person who made this book.

How are you feeling today?
Color the facial expressions that match your mood.

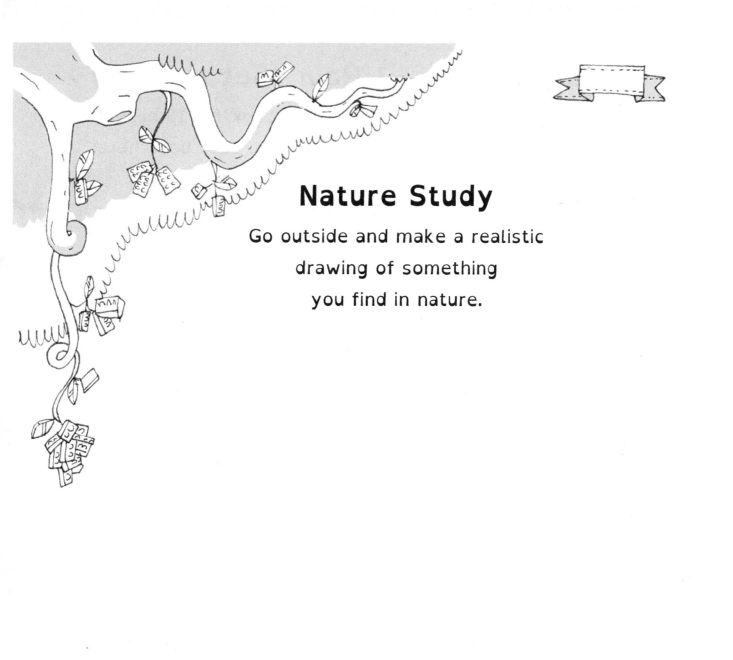

Nature Study

Go outside and make a realistic drawing of something you find in nature.

Reading Time - 1 Hour (Set a timer)

Choose Four Books - Read from each book for 15 minutes.

Copy important words or pictures from each book here:

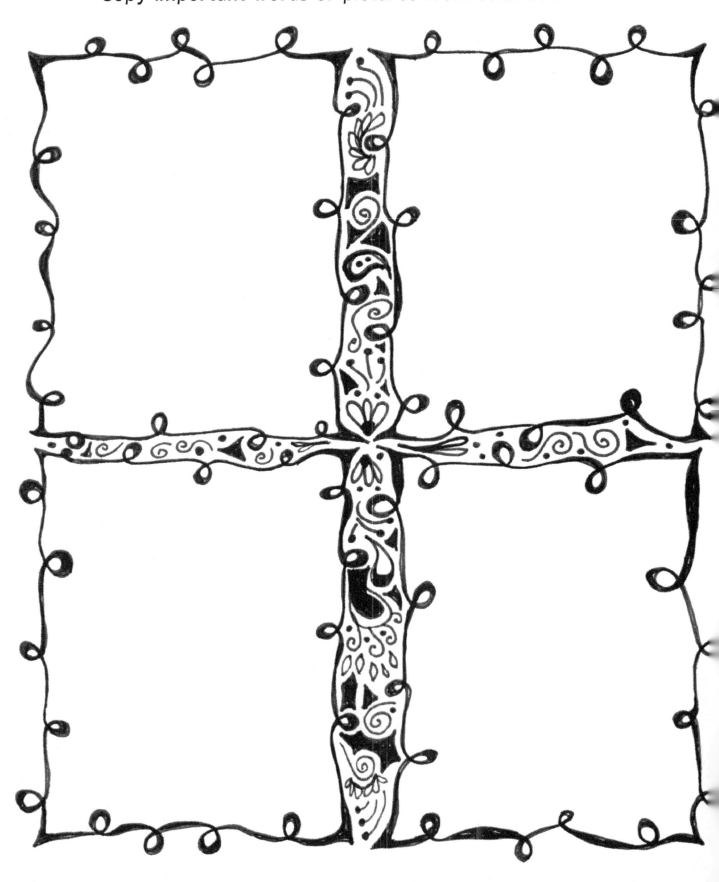

Spelling Time

Find 20 Words with 10 letters each.
Look in your books for words.
Write the words here:

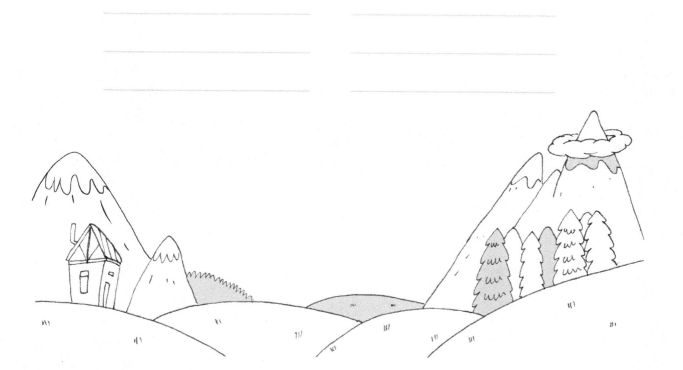

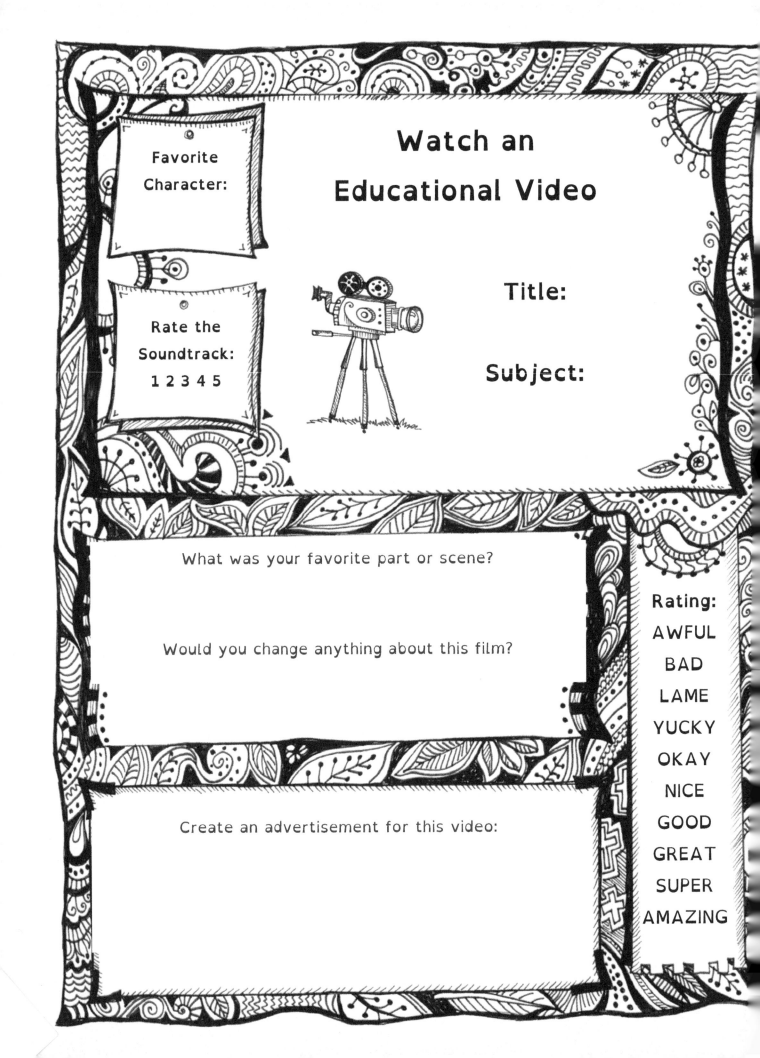

Use THIS PAGE for Math Practice

Or be creative and design something, like a house! You could make graphs, maps or geometric designs with this graph paper.

Book Time

Find an interesting sentence in one of your books and copy it. Draw a picture to go with the words.

TITLE:_____

Page Number:_____

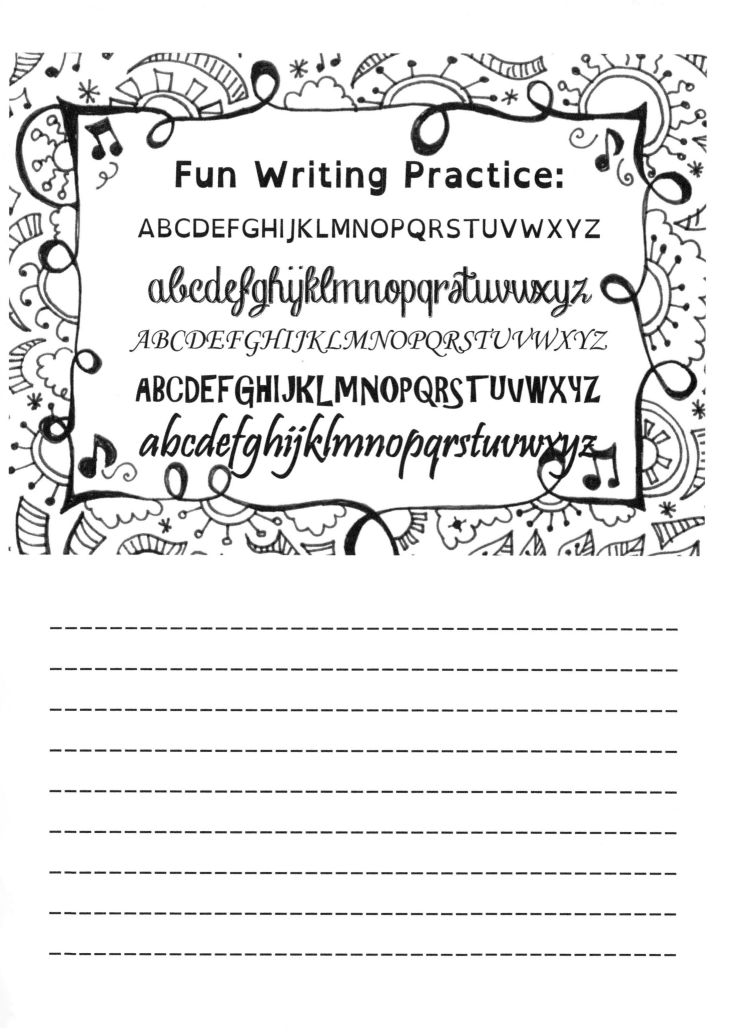

More Books!

More Books!

More Books!

Do It Yourself HOMESCHOOL JOURNALS

Copyright Information

Do It YOURSELF Homeschool Journal, and electronic printable downloads are for Home and Family use only. You may make copies of these materials for only the children in your household.

All other uses of this material must be permitted in writing by the Thinking Tree LLC. It is a violation of copyright law to distribute the electronic files or make copies for your friends, associates or students without our permission.

For information on using these materials for businesses, co-ops, summer camps, day camps, daycare, afterschool program, churches, or schools please contact us for licensing.

Contact Us:

The Thinking Tree LLC
617 N. Swope St. Greenfield, IN 46140. United States
317.622.8852 PHONE (Dial +1 outside of the USA) 267.712.7889 FAX
www.DyslexiaGames.com
jbrown@DyslexiaGames.com

Made in the USA
Coppell, TX
11 January 2022